KU-351-067

VIENNA

VIENNA

City of Dreams

Photographs by
Manfred Horvath
Text by
Käthe Springer

Verlag Christian Brandstätter · Vienna–Munich

DER · ZEIT · IHRE · KVNST ·
ER · KVNST · IHRE · FREIHEI

CONTENTS

The dome of gilded laurel leaves on the roof of the Secession – one of the landmarks of the city.

Previous double pages:

The giant Ferris Wheel by night.

The Lippizaner horses with their manes braided for a gala performance.

"All in all there all only two kinds of people on the earth – those who stay at home and those who don't," as Rudyard Kipling once wrote. But whether the adventure is one that takes place only in the mind or on site, so to speak, it's best to have a companion to provide you with everything you need for the journey of discovery: history and stories, information and pictures that help the city of your dreams to reveal itself to you with its heart and soul, with its emotions and its intellect.
Discover Vienna – or rather, rediscover Vienna. For the ancient city on the Danube has acquired a multiplicity of new faces. Today, Vienna is "in"; its incomparable collection of historical treasures, its long tradition of artistic creativity and its lively young cultural scene make the city one of the most loved and most popular destinations. After all, the wealth of sightseeing and cultural experiences that it has to offer is combined with both an excellent and varied choice of gastronomic delights and a modern night-life. Allow yourself to be seduced, enjoy this unique city as you find it in this book – full of charm but not without a little self-irony.

Welcome to Vienna!

Left:
A break during the Opera Ball.

Right:
In the "Dennstedt".

An overview of the history of Vienna

Vindobona – the Roman beginnings. The region around Vienna has been inhabited since prehistoric times. However, the city really began to exist in the year 15 BC, when the Romans penetrated into Celtic Noricum and constructed a defensive line, the Limes, along the Danube against the Germanic tribes. Their main camp was Carnuntum, located at the cross-roads of the Danube and the Amber Road from Poland to the Adriatic. To protect the flanks, Vindobona, an auxiliary camp, was established together with a civilian town on the present-day territory of Vienna – alongside a small Celtic settlement. The camp was destroyed around 400 AD by the Germanic tribes, but the Roman walls survived until the end of the 12th century (remains can still be seen at Hohenmarkt 3), providing protection to the developing settlement whose centre was located alongside the churches of St. Peter and Maria am Gestade north of the Hohenmarkt (Berghof with Ruprechtskirche). Fortified villages were built before the city gates, including trading settlements between the Wollzeile and the Fleischmarkt and on the site of the present-day Weihburggasse.

The Babenbergs. The end of the 12th century saw an expansion of the city. A new surrounding wall was built and was to define the development of Vienna for centuries. The settlement was first mentioned as civitas (town) in 1137, the church of St. Stephen was dedicated in 1147, and the Babenbergs, the first important dynasty on Austrian soil, took up residence in the ducal castle "Am Hof" in 1156. At the beginning of the 13th century, of the cities north of the Alps, Vienna was second in importance only to Cologne. Duke Leopold VI the Glorious proclaimed the first Vienna City Charter (1221), invited Catholic monks into the city (the Teutonic Order, the Dominicans, the Friars Minor), whose churches can still be seen today, and founded the Michaelskirche (St. Michael's Church). Vienna which already extended as far as the present-day Ringstrasse, developed into a major centre of trade and courtly culture. The Babenberg's magnificent "Hof ze Wienne" was witness to a blossoming of Minnesang (German troubadour music) and heroic epics, and the courtly amusements included knights tour-

naments and wandering minstrels. After this climax, Vienna began to descend into crisis under Friedrich II, the Belligerent. The duke fully lived up to his nickname, falling out with the rural aristocracy, the Viennese and the Church. He marched into Hungary without success, and came off worse in the dispute with his namesake Emperor Friedrich II. The Emperor was welcomed into Vienna and raised the city to the status of a free imperial city, making it directly subject to the Emperor and granting it a wide range of privileges. As "Kammerknechte", the Jewish population enjoyed the protection of the Emperor. He withdrew from the city a little less than three years later, leaving Vienna once again in the hands of Friedrich the Belligerent. The latter gave assistance to the Jews of the city by granting them special rights. He died in

The Neo-baroque St. Michael's dome above the St. Michael's wing of the Imperial Palace.

a fall from his horse in 1246 after his victory over the Hungarians at the Battle on the Leitha. Since he had no descendants, this was the end of the Babenbergs and Austria and Styria returned to the Empire. By this time the population of Vienna had grown to approx. 10 000.

The beginnings of the House of Habsburg. In 1273 a Habsburg, Rudolf I, became German King. In 1282, he granted his sons Albrecht and Rudolf "jointly" the duchies of Austria and Styria in fief, thereby founding Habsburg rule in these countries. From 1283 on, Albrecht reigned alone. In 1278, Vienna had won back from King Rudolf I the old civic charter, extended by certain privileges. Thus, the city council had been led by a mayor since 1282. However, Albrecht, now reigning alone, failed to confirm these rights, hitting the economic and political nerve of the middle classes. The result was an uprising that Albrecht had difficulty in defeating. In 1296, a considerably restricted civic charter limited the patricians' scope for political action, and made "the capital of the Empire in Austria" (Rudolf I) largely dependent on the sovereign, a relationship which was not to change for the whole of the Middle Ages. The Habsburgs extended the palace (the Swiss Wing of the Imperial Palace) and promoted the development of the aristocratic quarter (around the Herrengasse), but for a long time were unable to overcome the distrust of the Viennese. Nevertheless, since the beginning of the 14th century Vienna's priority over the other cities of the Habsburg territories was undisputed.

The oldest representation of Vienna: An extract from the panel painting "Meeting of Joachim and Anna", part of the Albrechtaltar, Klosterneuburg Monastery (around 1438).

Vienna until the end of the Middle Ages. Vienna soon proved to be a powerful magnet, with many settlements being created close by. They were all connected with the city by continuous roads, which both guaranteed their inhabitants protection in the event of danger and opened up markets for their products. Destroyed during the Turkish wars, these villages, the seeds of the later suburbs and outskirts soon sprang up again. One of these "connecting roads" is the Rennweg, which once lead from the city to the vineyards and small villages; its name derives from the "Scharlachrennen" (scarlet races), a popular festival that took place on the road from 1382 to 1534 at the same time as the two important fairs on Ascension Day and St. Catherine's Day (25.11). After the horse race, the young men and subsequently, to the general delight, the whores of the city came together for a race. The first prize was a scarlet cloth, from which the name of the festival derived.

The 14th century also saw the consolidation of Habsburg power. At the same time, the old city was expanded. St. Stephen's church was given a Gothic choir, the Augustinerkirche next to the Burg was built between 1330 and 1339, and the church of Maria am Gestade in 1330.

Duke Rudolf IV the Founder reigned from 1358 to 1365, and gave Vienna a new "capital city feeling": he laid the foundation stone for the tower of St. Stephen (1359), founded the University (1365), the second-oldest university in the German speaking world after Prague, and initiated significant economic and social reforms.

In 1396, the Habsburgs proclaimed a new city charter, the "Ratswahlprivileg", which put the Christian craftsmen and tradesmen on the same level as the patricians, thus putting an end to the dominance of the hereditary middle class. This interference in the "class struggle" saved the city – unlike many German cities – from bloody battles. In the 15th century, this imposed means of conflict avoidance, of course, no longer had much effect: any mayor who wanted to follow independent policies along the lines of German imperial cities paid dearly.

Thus Konrad Vorlauf was executed in 1408 for being on the losing side in the course of a Habsburg family quarrel, and Konrad Holzer, a darling of the people, met the same fate in 1436 as a result of unsuccessful political manoeuvrings. The year 1421, in the reign of Albrecht V, saw a monstrous persecution of the Jews (the Vienna Gesera) and the destruction of their district around the Judenplatz. In 1462, the citizens of Vienna laid siege to the Hofburg, in which Emperor Friedrich III and family had taken refuge during another Habsburg family crisis – and that despite his grant of a new coat of arms for their loyalty in 1461. And finally the Hungarian King, Matthias Corvinus, occupied the city from 1485 to 1490.

Vienna had not been particularly fortunate under Emperor Friedrich III, and little improved under his son Maximilian I (1493–1519). The city had felt mighty enough to face up to an emperor, but lost its economic and political significance under the policy of the son. It was little consolation that Maximilian founded the Hofmusikkapelle (Imperial Band) in 1498, and the "Kapellenknaben" choir, the precursors of the famous Vienna Boys' Choir. This could hardly make good the decline of the once magnificent imperial centre.

In 1517, Maximilian I granted Vienna a new city charter which allowed the Emperor considerable powers. This was the start of the period of absolute monarchy, a clear revocation of municipal autonomy. When Maximilian died in 1519, the two phenomena that were to shake Europe in the course of that century were already casting their shadows: the appearance of Martin Luther's new doctrines, and the threat from the Turks.

Circular plan of Vienna, woodcut by Niklas Meldeman (1530).

The First Turkish Siege. In 1529, the Turks under Sultan Suleiman II besieged the city for the first time, failing to capture it by only a hair's breadth – an event of more than local significance. The whole of Central Europe felt threatened, and Emperor Ferdinand I rapidly strengthened the old city fortifications. Following the Italian model, the following three decades saw the construction of modern fortifications in the Renaissance style, which would dominate the appearance of the city until they were razed in 1857. Outside the bastions and glacis lay the suburbs, the home of craftsmen and tradesmen, and, beyond these, the surrounding villages.

The Relief of Vienna in September 1683, painting by F. Greffels.

Reformation and counter-reformation. The conflict with the Protestants became increasingly virulent in the course of the 16th century. Under the tolerant Emperor Maximilian II, almost 80% of Vienna was Protestant in the 1570s and the city even had a Lutheran mayor for a short time – a unique case in the history of Catholic Vienna. Maximilian was followed by Rudolf II, whose transfer of the imperial residency to Prague temporarily cost Vienna its primacy.

The 17th century saw the victory of the Catholic counter-reformation. Numerous religious orders moved into Vienna, and almost all their churches are still standing today; in the suburbs these include the churches of the Carmelites (Leopoldstadt), the Augustinians (Landstrasse), the Friars of St. Paul (Wieden) and the Servites (Rossau), while the Franciscans, Dominicans and Capuchins (the Capuchin vault remained the burial place of the Habsburgs) established their churches in the inner city. The Schottenkirche (Church of the Scots) was given its Baroque appearance, and the imposing Jesuit church was built alongside the Old University run by the Jesuits.

The Thirty Years' War (1618–48) practically ignored Vienna, with the Swedes approaching only once, but not attacking. In 1624, the Jews were allocated a ghetto in what is today the Leopoldstadt, but were obliged to leave it again in 1670. It was another four years before 250 Jewish families were once again permitted to set up home in Vienna (for more on the history of the Viennese Jews.

The second Turkish siege. As the 17th century came to an end, Vienna was struck down by a catastrophic epidemic of the plague (1679), followed by the second Turkish siege of the city (1683). An army of 300,000 surrounded Vienna, hopelessly outnumbering the 17,000 defendants. It was only thanks to a "European" relief army, almost a quarter of which was Polish, that the city was finally saved. The Turks fled, leaving booty of inestimable value in the hands of the victors.

The "Baroque metropolis". However, this was not the end of the Ottoman threat to Vienna. It fell to the commander Prince Eugen, who had taken part in the relief battle as a solder, to force the Turkish army back to the Balkans over the following three decades, opening the gateway to the south-east to the Austrian Emperor. The frontier city of Vienna became the centre point of a huge empire.

The economic and cultural consequences of the military victories turned Vienna into a sparkling Baroque city equal to any in Europe in the 18th century, with art, music and theatre flourishing. The figureheads of this ascent are Leopold I (1659–1705), the first "Baroque Emperor", and Karl VI (1711–40), but above all the latter's daughter, Maria Theresia (1740–80), who had Schönbrunn palace extended and made Vienna the capital of an absolutist centralised state. Her son, Joseph II (1780–90) went down in history for his far-reaching reforms, including the Patent of Tolerance (1781), the dissolution of the monasteries (1782), a reform of the city government (1783) which completely revoked the city's autonomy, the promotion of science, technology and education, as well as the founding of the Hofburg theatre as the National Theatre (1776). Joseph II, who dreamed of a large empire with a centralised administration and German as its official language, eliminated the last remaining elements of municipal administration and thus founded the Austrian civil-service state. The effects of the enlightened absolutism named after him, Josephinism, continued into the 20th century.

Napoleon and the Congress of Vienna. In the meantime, the start of the new century was announced by the consequences of the French Revolution and Napoleon's claims to power. Napoleon occupied Vienna twice (1805 and 1809), taking up quarters in Schönbrunn. Despite the Austrian celebration of one of their few successes at the battle of Aspern (near Vienna), there was initially nothing to stop Napoleon's succession of victories. As a precautionary measure, Emperor Franz had already assumed the Austrian imperial crown in 1804, abdicating the Holy Roman crown in 1806; in 1810, following the traditional Habsburg policy on marriage, he gave his daughter Marie Louise in marriage to the mighty Frenchman. Of course, this did little to help the Viennese, who had been caused no end of trouble by the ravages of the war: there was a serious shortage of accommodation and prices rocketed. In 1811, the huge military expenditure led to a state bankruptcy and a collapse of the currency that took the Viennese economy over two decades to recover from.

But to outward appearances, the city remained as sparkling as ever: the Congress of Vienna met in 1814 and 1815, following the final down-fall of Napoleon, permitted the old powers to reorganise Europe under the leadership of Prince Metternich. "The Congress dances" was the later comment in the light of the countless magnificent celebrations that combined politics and pleasure. This was followed by the period of "Vormärz": police state, censorship, the removal of civil rights, social misery. The consequences were a disinterest in politics, a desire for pleasure, a withdrawal into private life – the "Biedermeier", as this culture of the disenfranchised middle class was later to be known (for more about the Biedermeier period.

The 1848 Revolution: "Barricade at Michaelerplatz", painting by Anton Ziegler.

The 1848 revolution. Despite the difficult conditions, industrialisation also reached suppressed Austria. Factories arose in Vienna's suburbs, the first steam ship was launched (1817), the first gas works were built in 1828 and the first railway line opened in 1837. The downside was the poor working conditions, low wages, appalling residential conditions and a total lack of political rights. The economic upheavals intensified the social and political conflicts, and culminated in the revolution of 1848, the first time that workers, students, the middle classes and peasants were united in bloody defeat.

The era of the Ringstrasse. The reign of Emperor Franz Joseph I (1848–1916) was a period of neo-absolutism. In 1850 the suburbs (up to today's Gürtel) were in-

Panorama of the extended city of Vienna, colour drawing by G. Veith (around 1873).

corporated into the city which, with its population of now 431,000, was divided into 8 districts. The next expansion of the city followed in 1857. On the orders of Emperor Franz Joseph, the city walls were demolished and the surrounding glacis built over. Where the walls had once stood, the leading architects of Europe created today's Ringstrasse – a unique major urban development project. The 1860s and '70s also saw improvements to the infrastructure: the first water-pipeline from Alpine springs was constructed, the Danube was regulated, the Central Cemetery and the city park were created. In 1890 the outskirts (outside today's Gürtel) became part of Vienna. Even while this new expansion of the city was being put into practice, the office of mayor fell to a controversial politician, Karl Lueger (1844–1910), Christian-Social by persuasion, authoritarian, witty and deeply anti-Semitic. It was under Lueger that Vienna became the modern metropolis: the municipal gas and electricity works were constructed, the trams were taken over by the city and electrified, the second water pipeline from the Alpine springs was built, the forest and green belt round the city was set up, and measures were taken in the field of social affairs and health. In 1905, Floridsdorf, on the left bank of the Danube, became part of the city, and soon the population had passed the 2 million mark. However, in the expanding capital and imperial residence of the huge multiethnic state, there was growing popular unrest. Vienna was attracting more and more people from all parts of the monarchy in their search for work – an explosive mix of peoples rather than the peaceful "melting pot" into which modern memory seems to have transformed it. Otto Wagner, Adolf Loos and many others were active in the field of architecture, while the Second Viennese School of Medicine achieved world-wide fame through celebrated doctors such as Theodor Billroth and Joseph Skoda. Sigmund Freud was also active in Vienna at that time, although his achievements only found recognition much later. Musicians, poets, painters, philosophers – they all marked this era of the fin-de-siècle, which, supported by the nobility, achieved legendary fame.

Red Vienna. The First World War broke out in 1914, and by the time it reached its end, nothing was ever to be the same again. The monarchy had collapsed, the Habsburgs had been banished, Austria had shrunk from a huge multi-ethnic state into a tiny republic that no-one gave any chance of survival. Resources and markets had been lost. Vienna, much too large for this country, had become a huge head dominated by hunger, shortage of accommodation and poverty together with an inflated bureaucracy. In 1919, the franchise was extended to everyone, and in the elections that followed the Social Democrats won an absolute majority in the city council, a majority they have retained to the present (only violently interrupted from 1934 to 1938 by Austro-fascism, and from 1938 to 1945 by National Socialism). Vienna became an independent federal province in 1922, thus separating it from Lower Austria. The city's achievements from then until 1934 – undeterred by state repression and the global economic crises – in the fields of municipal residential construction, social affairs and health, made "Red Vienna" world famous.

The rise of fascism. However, the internal political contradictions and social conflicts came to a head, erupting in the bloody civil war of February 1934, the first battle between democratic and fascist forces in Europe. Victory went to Austro-fascism under Federal Chancellor Engelbert Dollfuss, putting an end to Vienna's reconstruction activities. Karl Seitz, the Social-Democratic Burgermeister, was – like many Viennese at the time – arrested, and the city council was dissolved and replaced by a corporation that was no longer freely elected.

National Socialism. In March 1938, the authoritarian regime merged smoothly into the Anschluss of Austria with Hitler's Germany and the National Socialist reign of terror. A new wave of arrests eliminated or at least weakened political opponents. Thousands of Viennese were persecuted for political, racial, ethical or religious reasons. The Jewish element of the population was practically entirely wiped out, as were the ethnic groups of the Roma and the Sinti. Almost all the synagogues were destroyed. Vienna also suffered serious damage from allied bombing, with St. Stephan's, the symbol of Vienna, falling victim to the flames as the city was liberated by the Allies in April 1945.

The post war period. Divided into a British, Russian, American, and French zone, Vienna remained under military occupation until Austria's independence in 1955 – as well as becoming a market place for smugglers (remember The Third Man) and a centre for international espionage.

Vienna today. In the years that followed, Vienna, thanks to its location and history, found itself in the role of commercial, political and cultural mediator between East and West. Today it is a city of congresses as well as the headquarters of

The modern face of Vienna: IBM building by the architect Wilhelm Holzbauer.

the United Nations and other international organisations.

The whole of the centre of Vienna, the inner city with its historic buildings, is classified as an historic monument. Nevertheless, Vienna is not a museum. The opening of eastern Europe in 1989 and membership of the European Union in 1995 brought additional life into the city, presenting it with new tasks and perspectives, and a new responsibility as the interface between East and West.

Art and Culture

Vienna,
the Cultural Metropolis

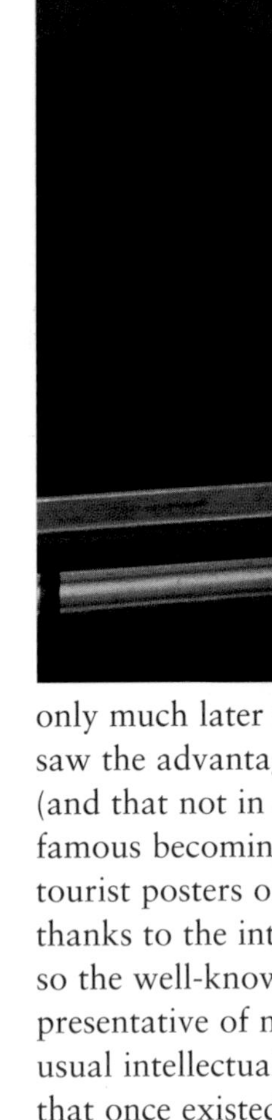

"The streets of Vienna are plastered with culture, the streets of other cities with asphalt", as Karl Kraus once sneered. But this great linguistic and cultural critic could not have predicted that his contribution to the Viennese Modern has long made him an element of the city's cultural image, an image which, together with the imperial inheritance of the city of the emperors, has now become an attraction for a world-wide audience.

Vienna at the turn of the century, an era that was the creative stimulus for art, culture and science, was bursting with great figures who have now (almost) acquired the status of brand names: Sigmund Freud, Gustav Klimt, Egon Schiele, Adolf Loos, Ludwig Wittgenstein, Arnold Schönberg, Gustav Mahler, Karl Kraus, Arthur Schnitzler and many more – without doubt a powerful team. But the city to whose cultural revival these artists, writers, architects, composers, philosophers and scientists contributed so much, has not always been so proud of them as it is today. In many cases their works encountered extreme hostility and rejection – or were snubbed according to the ancient Viennese principle of "not even ignoring" them. Thanks to their Jewish origin, many of those mentioned were later to fall victim to National Socialism, were murdered or finally banished, ultimately achieving in exile the fame and recognition that had been denied them at home. It was only much later that their home country saw the advantage of remembering them (and that not in all cases), with the most famous becoming export hits, figures on tourist posters or gaining popularity thanks to the interest from abroad ... And so the well-known names are always representative of many phenomenon, the unusual intellectual productivity and variety that once existed in this city despite every-

Previous double page:
View from the National Theatre to the Town Hall Square, where the summer evening films are shown.

Below:
Gustav Klimt's "The Kiss", the symbol of Viennese Jugendstil.

thing, their own banishment and extermination – and finally their slow and gradual re-discovery. Whatever might have been the reasons for this return to favour, it brought to the light of day the enormous intellectual potential that plays a major contribution to Vienna's international reputation as a cultural city.
Of course, Vienna has more to offer those interested in culture than what was created at the turn of the century when the days of the monarchy were already numbered. *Vienna Gloriosa* – the significance and radiation of the still mighty capital and residence of the Danube monarchy that is manifested in the rich treasures of architecture, art and music – is much more the real attraction for thousands and thousands of visitors. Those who want can indeed view Vienna through the spectacles of magnifi-

Treasury: The Austrian Imperial Crown with Sceptre and Orb, on the wall Friedrich Amerling's painting of Emperor Franz I.

The new Haas House on Stephansplatz (architect Hans Hollein) has become one of the sights of Vienna.

cence: imposing Gothic, excessive Baroque, the imperial gesture of the Habsburg power turned to stone. Those who mourn the imperial and royal past will find plenty to meet their taste. But even in the most pathetic touches it will still be possible to see a colourful entourage of sharp-tongued critics, imaginative and enchanting dreamers and coarsely humorous folksiness – that mixture of traditional Viennese and "immigrants" that has always been the mark of Viennese culture. "Vienna is both", the Viennese author Hans Weigel once wrote in a "critical declaration of love" to the city, referring to ambivalence as one of the features of the city. "You can write whatever you want about Vienna, it will always be true." This is not meant to imply arbitrariness but rather the inner conflicts, the contradictions – not only of the Viennese soul but also of Viennese history and culture. It may be that this is also true to a certain extent of other cities, but for Vienna it has been and remains true to a very particular extent.

Austria's capital has remained "a faithful nest of contradictions" (Ernst Stein) to the present day. While in certain quarters the insults, carping, intrigues, ignoring, doubts and pessimism have never ended, the calm of the post-war period, the return to traditions and a gradual revitalisation of what was previously disowned and suppressed have led to a resurgence in Vienna's cultural activity. The old is being rediscovered. What in Austria is called "high culture" and mainly refers to the classical tradition, is indeed maintained at a high and internationally recognised level. Alongside it, a mercurial avant-garde has developed, bring-ing new stimuli into many areas and scenes.

Vienna is once again in the process of acquiring many faces. This is to be welcomed and is ground for hope. It seems indeed to be the case that Vienna, the cultural metropolis that has for so long been happy to live off its past, has now added a lively presence, and – as it seems – a lively future.

ARCHITECTURE

The Stephansdom (St. Stephen's Cathedral), Schönbrunn Palace and the Hundertwasserhaus are amongst the most popular public attractions of Viennese architecture. And it is in precisely this sequence that they represent major eras of Viennese architectural history, from the Gothic via Baroque to contemporary architecture. Of course, there is plenty in between – Biedermeier, Historicism or Jugendstil – and the architectural appearance of the city is much more complex than could be represented by just three styles. Yet this popular trio covers decisive periods, revealing them to the visitor to Vienna in all their variety. Medieval alleys, Gothic spires, Baroque palaces, sleepy Biedermeier court-yards – from time immemorial, the capital and residence of the Danube Monarchy occupied a central position in matters concerning art and architecture. Much has survived, standing alongside the buildings of the inter-war period and the architecture of today – a true "collage of the centuries", as one writer on architecture put it.

Romanesque (10th–12th centuries). In addition to the Ruprechtskirche (St. Rupert's Church), the oldest church in the city, the only stone reminders of the first cultural climax of Vienna under the Babenbergs are a few original parts of St. Stephen's Cathedral (Giant's Gate) and the Heidentürme (Towers of the Heathens), and the core of the Schweizertrakt (Swiss Wing) in the Imperial Palace (Hofburg), the repository of every style up to Historicism.

Gothic (12th–14th centuries). The Gothic period saw a blossoming of architecture. Delicate pointed arches, slender columns and flying buttresses, elegant vaults and high naves are its main features, while its most important representative is the Stephansdom, a Gothic construction of European significance. The huge interior and the south tower, which was to become the symbol of the city, testified to the wealth of the middle classes and glorified the power of the Habsburgs. The Church of Maria am Gestade is an other Gothic jewel. However, most buildings from this period were altered during the Baroque period or subsequently, often fitted with a new facade, such as the late Romanesque/early Gothic Michaelerkirche (St. Michael's Church), once the court church of the Babenbergs, or the three-nave hall church "Zu den neun Chören der Engel" (The Nine Choirs of Angels). Even the Augustinerkirche (Augustinian Church) with its high-gothic appearance is no longer original, but was re-gothicised at the end of the 18th century, as

View from the "Holy Ghost Hole" of the main nave of St. Stephen's Cathedral.

was the Minoritenkirche (Church of the Friars Minor).

Renaissance (16th century). Unfortunately nothing survives of the largest Viennese building project of the Renaissance, the city fortifications. And it would seem that the construction of the fortifications according to an Italian model hardly left any money or labour for other buildings. Moreover, the Renaissance Prince par excellence, Emperor Rudolf II, resided in Prague and not Vienna, which is why the architecture of this period has left fewer traces on the city. The Stallburg and the Neugebäude Palace (both built for Emperor Maximilian II) are the two most important Renaissance buildings of Vienna, reflecting in their facades reason, humanity and the liberal spirit of antiquity. However, the Stallburg with its magnificent arcade court-yard (inside the Hofburg) was converted into stables in 1565, only one year after it was completed, and in the 18th century became the home of the famous Lipizzaner stallions of the Spanish Riding School. The Neu-gebäude hunting palace (near today's Central Cemetery), built in the years following 1569, was a unique building for the Europe of the time, with a huge park containing magnificent garden terraces, a chapel, a view tower and an underground grotto. But the castle fell into decay under Maria Theresia, and parts were used to build Schönbrunn Palace and in particular the Gloriette. In the 19th century, the garden was used as an urn grove and thus became part of the Central Cemetery.

View of the Lower Belvedere.

Baroque (17th century). After the plague was overcome and the Habsburgs had defeated the Turks and the Reformation, the culture of the Catholic nobility at the turn of the 17th and 18th centuries experienced a triumphal climax. Display was everything, spirituality little. A construction boom began, started by the Emperor and the Church, and continued by the aristocracy, manifesting itself in magnificent winter palaces in the inner city and splendid summer residences in the suburbs constructed by star architects. Playful lightness and exuberant joie de vivre reflect the achievements of this period in the field of applied art. It is the era of the great architects, of Johann Lukas von Hildebrandt (1668–1745), Johann Bernhard Fischer von Erlach (1656–1723) and his son Joseph Emmanuel. Hildebrandt created a style of architecture that lives from the wealth of architectural elements and ornaments and the play of light and shade, such as in the Upper Belvedere Palace (1721–22). He was also responsible for the Lower Belvedere Palace, the Secret Court and State Chancellery (today the office of the Federal Chancellor) and the Piaristenkirche (Church of the Piarists). In contrast, the style of his rival, J. B. Fischer von Erlach, is marked by flat surfaces and strict structures (e.g. the Imperial Library, 1732–35) and massive monumentality (e.g. the Karlskirche (St. Charles' Church) 1716–39). His most famous building is Schönbrunn Palace, which was converted for Maria Theresia by Nicolaus Pacassi (1716–90) in 1744–49, and its interior decoration ranks it as the most impressive creation of the Viennese Rococo. G.E. Fischer von Erlach continued his father's building projects, but also created significant works of his own such as the Imperial Chancery Wing and the Winter Riding School in the Hofburg. Contributions to Viennese Rococo also came from many Austro-Italian architects such as Carlo Canevale, Andrea del Pozzo and Carlo Antonio Carlone.

Rococo (18th century). From 1743 on, Nicolaus Pacassi, Vienna's star Rococo architect, carried out fundamental alterations on the Hetzendorf Hunting Palace, presumably constructed by Hildebrandt;

today it is home to the Vienna School of Fashion. Vienna's most striking Rococo construction is the Great Hall of the Old University.

Biedermeier (1st half of the 19th century). This period between the Congress of Vienna and the 1848 Revolution saw the construction of many of the attractive romantic middle-class houses that in part still survive today. The outstanding architect of the time was Josef Kornhäusel (1782–1860), who was responsible for the Ceremonial Hall in the Hofburg, the synagogue at Seitenstettengasse 4 and the re-building of the Schottenstift (Monastery of the Scots). His home, the Kornhäusel Turm, is located in Baden bei Wien, like so many of his buildings, which continue to determine the appearance of this spa resort.

Historicism (2nd half of the 19th century). Historicism became the decisive art-style after 1848 – an eclectic style that imitated all the styles of the past. The up-and-coming period of promoterism, which turned Vienna into the modern metropolis it is today, saw the construction of numerous public representational buildings in the style of past eras. It is above all the ostentatious buildings along the new Ringstrasse (from 1857) that are the symbol of this period. The Opera House, the Academy of Fine Arts, the Museum of Art, the Natural History Museum, the Parliament Building, the Town Hall, the National Theatre, the University, the Stock Exchange, etc. line cheek by jowl – like a "museum of architecture" – this magnificent boulevard, no doubt the most important in Europe in terms of urban architecture. At the same time, architects such as Theophil Hansen, Heinrich Ferstel, Gottfried Semper, Carl Hasenauer, Friedrich Schmidt, August Sicard von Sicardsburg and Eduard van der Nüll also created works away from the Ringstrasse, such as the Neo-gothic Votivkirche (Votive Church) and the Church of

The Albertina ramp (with the equestrian statue of Archduke Albrecht to the right) provides an excellent view of the State Opera House.

Maria vom Siege, the castle-like Arsenal, now the home of the Military Museum, the Musikverein building, whose Golden Hall is the venue for the annual New Year's Concert by the Vienna Philharmonic Orche-stra, or the pavilions of the Freudenau race-track.

Jugendstil (turn of the 19th/20th centuries). A major break took place shortly before the turn of the century: led by Otto Wagner (1841–1918), who as early as 1885 had emphasised the technical and objective side of building in, for instance the entire architectural structure of the urban railway system, the so called Secessionists rose up in protest against traditional forms of architectural expression. The Modern was beginning. The new aesthetic ideal, a symbiosis of function and ornament, gave birth to the style known as Jugenstil, some of whose representatives also achieved considerable success in the field of applied art. Wagner's buildings, including the Postsparkasse (Post Office Savings Bank), the Church am Steinhof and a number of villas, are pioneer works of modern architecture. Likewise, Joseph Olbrich (Secession), Friedrich Ohmann (regulation of the Wien river) and Josef Hoffmann (the Prukersdorf Sanatorium) were revolutionary in their use of functionality and simple ornamentation. Adolf Loos (1870–1933) was a radical purist who played a special role as uncompromising pioneer of extreme functionalism and austere designs. His theoretical writings *(Ornament und Verbrechen, 1908)*, designs and buildings (the house on the Michaelerplatz, the Loos Bar, a number of villas) were a model for all following generations. His demand for functionalism is reflected in the inter war period in the Werkbund estate, in the planning of the large council houses, and indeed in the design of the "Frankfurt kitchen" (the first fitted kitchen) by the Viennese Margarete Schütte-Lihotzky, one of his former co-workers.

Dome of the Church am Steinhof by Otto Wagner.

Red Vienna (1919–34). After the collapse of the monarchy and the proclamation of the republic, Vienna lost its position as the capital of a huge multi-ethnic state. The powerful labour movement led by the Austro-Marxists resulted in the electoral victory of the Social Democrats in 1919. And when Vienna became a separate federal province in 1922, the social reforms of "Red Vienna" began to take shape. Thus by 1934, with the assistance of countless famous architects, the large apartment complexes, surrounded by green and yet of almost defensive appearance, had been constructed for the destitute population. Typical examples are one-kilometre-long Karl Marx Hof (Döbling), the mighty and massive Reumann-Hof (Favoriten) or the spacious Sandleitenhof (Ottakring) – impressive testimony to a unique socio-political and architectural experiment.

Post war period. The long architectural recession during the world economic crisis and Austro-fascism (1934–38), and the destruction caused by the Second World War, were followed in the years immediately after 1945 by artistic stagnation. Acute lack of accommodation, reconstruction and economic need left no space for creativity. And even in later years the new generation of architects failed to achieve the pre-war standards of the Modern. The few large building projects of this period include the Stadthalle (Roland Rainer), the Church "Zur Heiligsten Dreifaltigkeit"

Vienna is moving upwards – with the Andromeda Tower (left) and the Vienna International Centre ("UNO City") on the left bank of the Danube.

(The Most Holy Trinity) in the district of Mauer by Fritz Wotruba, and the 20er Haus (Karl Schwanzer), part of the Ludwig Foundation of the Museum of Modern Art, Vienna. It was only in the 1960s (Wilhelm Holzbauer, Gustav Peichl, Hans Hollein) and the 1970s (Hermann Czech, Coop Himmelb(l)au, Missing Link, Hausrucker & Co) that the Viennese architectural scene experienced a new start and an initial opening-up to the outside world. Alongside the Vienna International Centre, this period's major construction was the United Nations' City (Johann Staber, 1973) near the Danube Island, home to the United Nations' world headquarters for crime prevention, drugs control and atomic energy, as well as the UNIDO. Nowadays, architectural pluralism sets the tone, and Vienna boasts a wide variety of styles such as the ingenious shapes of the Postmodernist star Hans Hollein (e.g. the Haas Haus, 1985–90), the new "Classicism" of Rob Krier (e.g. the residential building in the 10th district, Schrankenberggasse 18–20, constructed in 1983), the Coop Himmelb(l)au Group's deconstructivism (e.g. the Reiss Bar, 1977) or the ecological buildings of Friedensreich Hundertwasser (e.g. the Hundertwasserhaus, 1983–85). A new generation has taken over in the 1990s, reinterpreting the relationship to the Modern, and largely involved in the construction of homes and schools, shop architecture and the design of bars and restaurants (BKK-2, Maria Auböck, Eichinger or Knechtl). At the same time, the old garde is involved in major projects such as the skyscrapers of the "Danube City" in the 22nd District, or the conversion of the old Messepalast into the "Museum Quarter". Even a short stroll through the city shows that Vienna has developed over the centuries into one of the most beautiful European metropolises, and that the city, despite all quarrels and scandals, is today making every effort not only to maintain its extremely valuable historical architecture, but also to allow modern architecture to develop.

Fine Arts

"Here, we particularly appreciate painting on cakes", scoffed Karl Kraus, fortunately not a quotation that is valid for all times, as will be seen below.

Leaving aside finds from the Celtic and Roman periods and early Medieval glass and altar painting (Vienna's only Romanesque glass paintings are in the middle choir window of the Ruprechtskirche (St. Rupert's Church)), our attention is drawn above all by three works of the **Gothic** period: the portrait of the Habsburg Duke Rudolf IV (1365), considered to be the oldest portrait created north of the Alps (today in the Cathedral and Diocesan Museum); the Neidhard Frescos (around 1400), the oldest secular wall paintings of Vienna, and the Schottenaltar (Altar of the Scots) (1469), whose surviving 21 panels show the earliest views of Vienna that can be interpreted topographically (in the museum of the Schottenstift). With his preference for naturalistic landscape and city paintings, the so called Scottish master was a precursor of the Danube School that developed around 1500 in the Vienna region. In sculpture too, indications of the work to come were already being created, as the Stephansdom shows: e.g. the "Dienstbotenmadonna" (Madonna of the Serving Maid) or the tomb of Friedrich III, an early precursor of the Renaissance; another interesting example of Gothic sculpture is the pulpit created by Anton Pilgram in 1515, in which he has immortalised himself in the very Viennese pose of a curious "Peeping Tom".

The stone mason Anton Pilgram left his own portrait in stone below the organ of St. Stephen's Cathedral.

The fine arts reached their climax in the **Baroque**. Highly esteemed masters such as Johann Michael Rottmayr and Daniel Gran, Franz Anton Maulbertsch, Paul Troger and Andrea del Pozzo gave full rein to their imagination in their ceiling frescos and altar paintings. Amongst the outstanding sculptors were Georg Raphael Donner (the Donner – actually the Providentia – fountain on the New Market), Balthasar Permoser and Balthasar Moll.

During the **Biedermeier** period, painting became particularly popular, with its tendency toward realism, carefulness and contemplation, and its preference for smaller formats ideal for decorating the home. The painting of the Biedermeier period is the artistic transformation of middle-class existence. Engravings and lithographic

The restorer Stöber working on Gustav Klimt's Beethoven Frieze in the Secession.

reproductions helped to disseminate art and put an end to the exclusiveness of its enjoyment. Genre paintings, intimate landscapes and views of Vienna, portraits and miniatures, were the preferred types. Masters such as Ferdinand Georg Waldmüller, Friedrich Gauermann, Peter Fendi and Rudolf von Alt acquired a European-wide reputation.
Like no other painter, Hans Makart (1840–84) completely dominated the style of his period. His large-scale paintings full of theatrical colour and sumptuous luxury, his opulent way of life, his sumptuous parties made him the star and trend-setter of Ringstrasse society during the period of **Historicism**.
The Vienna Secession movement was founded in 1897 as a reaction against traditional art activity and the fashionable popularity of Makart, and was based on the idea that art "should show modern man his true face" (Otto Wagner). In 1898, this protest movement, which was to give rise to the **Jugendstil**, acquired its own exhibition centre in the form of the Secession building constructed by Joseph Maria Olbrich. As its leader, they elected Gustav Klimt (1862–

1918), whose ornamental and decorative style broke the mould of historicism. His most popular works are *The Kiss* (1907/1908, displayed in the Austrian Gallery in the Upper Belvedere) and the *Beethoven Frieze* (1902), an extraordinary representation of the contents of Beethoven's *ninth symphony*.

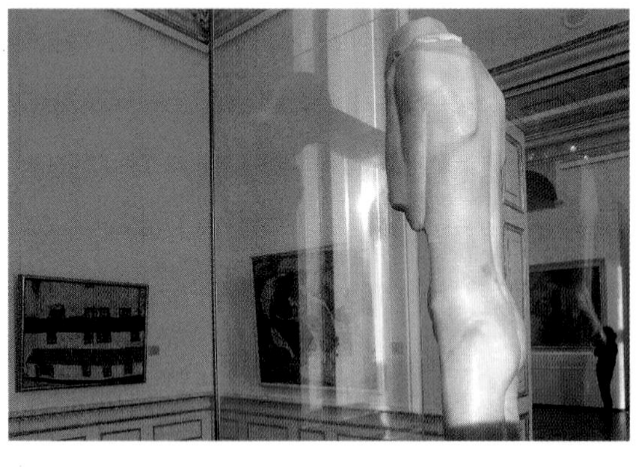

Schiele Room in the Austrian Gallery in the Upper Belvedere.

Even before the turn of the century, Klimt's contemporary Anton Romako, an outsider in terms of style, whose individualistic pioneering art made him one of the precursors of the modern, announced the arrival of **Expressionism**. This style finally achieved success through the works of Alfred Kubin, Egon Schiele, Richard Gerstl and Oskar Kokoschka.

The period of **National Socialism** was also an era of barbarism in art, and left behind an intellectual desert. Almost the entire cultural elite was wiped out or driven into exile. Art that did not fit into the dominant ideology was persecuted as degenerate, and in its place was propagated the ideology of "blood and soil" of popular art, purified "of unhealthy experiment". A travelling exhibition entitled *Degenerate Art* attracted 147,000 visitors in Vienna and included amongst its warning examples nine works by Oskar Kokoschka, a monstrous confirmation of the citation by Kraus at the beginning of this section, and one that was by no means at an end with the defeat of the Nazis in 1945.

One of the central personalities of artistic life in the **post-war period** was Herbert Boeckl (1894–1966). In the 1920s, he had been a main representative of Austrian Expressionism in painting, and after the Second World War this influential artist and professor at the Academy initiated a revival of religious art. Like Boeckl, Fritz Wotruba (1907–75) was a teacher and a father-figure of the artistic scene of the time in Vienna. Like his pupil Alfred Hrdlicka, Wotruba is one of the most important sculptors of the 20th century. His monumental stone figures set new criteria for the representation of physical harmony and established a school that was to determine the image of Austrian sculpture for many years to come. In 1976, the Church on the Georgenberg in the Mauer district of Vienna was completed according to his designs, a building made up of interlocked concrete blocks piled up on one another, transcending the limits between sculpture and architecture. One of the most exciting and productive chapters of Austrian artistic activity in the post-war period was written by the Art Club, founded in Vienna in 1947 and later acquir-ing the status of a myth. A collection of young painters, sculptors, authors and musicians, many of whom are today important artists, joined the group as a non-academic progressive "pack", and, like the Secessionists, sought international contacts. Their exemplary exhibitions caused a stir in the rigid, conservative Vienna of the time. Until 1953 the club occupied premises in the legendary "Strohkoffer" in the cellar of the Loos Bar; paintings by Friedensreich Hundertwasser and

Josef Mikl hung on the walls, Friedrich Gulda improvised on the piano, H.C. Artmann recited Garcia Lorca. The first President of the Art Club was Albert Paris Gütersloh (1887–1973), who even during his life time had become the cult figure of the Viennese avant-garde. He was a gifted multitalent – director, stage-designer, actor, author and painter in one, and his decorative realism determined the style for a large number of his pupils who were to become famous under the name *Fantastic Realists*. The Viennese School of *Fantastic Realism* included Ernst Fuchs, Rudolf Hausner, Anton Lehmden, Arik Brauer and Wolfgang Hutter. The style is a late Austrian version of Classical Surrealism, and was one of the most individualistic manifestations of the post-war scene, with an influence that still reverberates in fashionable circles. Although looked down upon by many critics, it was the first major Austrian style of art after 1945.
It was around this time that other important representatives of the post-war generation began their work, including painters such as Josef Mikl, Arnulf Rainer, Maria Lassnig, Oswald Oberhuber, Adolf

View from Heldenplatz of the New Palace; in the foreground the equestrian statue of Prince Eugen.

Museum of the 20th Century (architect Karl Schwanzer), in the foreground a sculpture by Rudolf Hoflehner.

Frohner and Christian Ludwig Attersee, the sculptor Alfred Hrdlicka (he created the Monument against War and Fascism on the Albertina Platz) and the most famous amongst the general public, Friedensreich Hundertwasser.

In the **1960s** artists such as Hermann Nitsch, Gunter Brus, Rudolf Schwarz-kogler, Otto Mühl, Valie Export and Peter Weibl shocked the world with provocative happenings, with actions involving the slaughter of animals, self-painting and self-mutilation. Rejecting all standards and constraints, they announced the destruction of all traditional conventions of expression, replacing them with "direct art". The *Viennese Actionists* were not concerned with art but with life (their own), subjective reality, pure perception and pure experience. Almost all the representatives of this initially persecuted style of art are now well known exponents of art and cultural life.

The **1970s** were dominated by conceptual art, social commitment, performances, feminist art and the transcendence of borders in the direction of dance, music etc. It was only in the **1980s** that interest once more focused on painting. For the first time contemporary art achieved astro-nomical prices, alongside the works of the Classical Modern. It became socially acceptable. Hubert Schmalix was the most successful painter, while the professor of the Academy and sculptor Bruno Gironcoli was an admired model. "The sun never stops shining for our fine art" is how the then mayor of Vienna, Helmut Zilk, described the change of climate in Vienna, which was otherwise generally more interested in music and theatre. The boom in art was followed by a new culture of life, with cafes, restaurants and vernissages as the places to meet, shooting up like mushrooms.

In the **1990s**, the artistic scene changed from being a society event and a label for politics and business and art became more oriented towards groups, events, and youth culture.

Computer networks and new media have become increasingly important, blurring the distinction from other areas. At the same time there has been an expansion of the infrastructure: the artistic scene is populated by critics, custodians, art magazines, galleries and exhibition rooms. Franz West is regarded as a link between the older and the younger generations. Originally one of the Actionists, today, with Arnulf Rainer, his body-related and even usable sculptures have made him undoubtedly the Austrian artist most frequently exhibited around the world. The young artists of the 1980s (including Hubert Scheibl, Herbert Brandl, Erwin Bohatsch, Peter Kogler, Walter Obholzer and Brigitte Kowanz, whose light in-stallations created a sensation), have also long achieved international success. For the first time since the monarchy, the creation of art is once again in the international lime light. Vienna has become part of the *global village* of contemporary art.

Museums, Galleries and Exhibition rooms

If not perhaps a museum itself, Vienna is in any event *the* city of museums. The list covers venerable collections and district museums, major exhibition houses of modern art and special collections such as the Tramway and Lipizzaner Museums. It would require too much space to list the curiosities such as the Museums of Bricks, of Hackney Cabs or of Horseshoes. Almost everyone, from the dog-lover to the football fan will find a collection in Vienna. In total over 120 public and private collections, memorials and museums of all kinds are open to visitors, frequently in a historical setting and with valuable exhibits. Some of these are among the best the world has to offer: the Albertina, the world's most important collection of graphic arts, the Museum of Fine Arts, one of the most famous collections of paintings in the world, as well as the Secular and Ecclesiastical Treasury, with exhibits of unique value both in artistic and in historical terms. They all owe their treasures to centuries of collecting and thieving by the art-loving Habsburgs. It is hardly surprising that for a time there was a rumour that there were more museum attendants than museum visitors in Vienna. But it isn't true. Since the start of a new boom in art in the 1980s, more attention is being paid to attracting the public: Old buildings such as the Secession, the Museum of Applied Art, the Albertina, the Austrian Gallery and the Treasury have been and are being renovated and fitted with shops and cafes, while new exhibition rooms have been and are being created, including the (temporary) Kunsthalle (Art Hall) on the Karlsplatz, the Kunstforum Vienna, Hundertwasser's KunstHaus Vienna or the "Museum Quarter".

The museums most worth seeing

Erzbischöfliches Dom- und Diözesanmuseum (Archiepiscopal Cathedral and Diocesan Museum). Seven centuries of religious art: paintings from the Gothic to Viennese Romanticism, reliquaries, religious objects, Gothic panel paintings, sculptures. Highlight: the portrait of Duke Rudolf IV, the

Weapon's Collection of the Museum of Fine Arts in the Imperial Palace.

oldest German portrait. 1st District, Stephansplatz 6 (passageway); Tel. 515 52-3689; Tuesdays–Saturdays, 10.00–17.00, except public holidays.
Gemäldegalerie der Akademie der bildenden Künste (Picture Gallery of the Academy of Fine Arts). No other academy of art possesses such a rich and impressive collection of master works dating from the

Part of the hologram on the Jewish history of Vienna in the Jewish Museum.

14th century to the present. Main aspects: early Dutch (Hieronymus Bosch, the Last Judgement altar piece), 17th century Flemish and Dutch (Rubens, van Dyck, Rembrandt, Pieter de Hooch), Austrian and Italian Baroque (Gran, Maulbertsch, Tiepolo) and works by teachers at the academy, from Füger and Waldmüller to Boeckl and Wotruba. 1st District, Schillerplatz 3; Tel. 588 16-0; Tuesdays, Thursdays, Fridays, 10.00–14.00, Wednesdays 10.00–13.00 and 15.00–18.00, Saturdays, Sundays, public holidays 9.00–13.00
Graphische Sammlung Albertina (Albertina Collection of Graphic Arts). Its 44,000 drawings and water colours and 1.5 million prints make the Albertina the most important collection of graphic arts in the world. Every artist from the beginning of the 15th century to the present, including masterpieces by Leonardo da Vinci, Michelangelo. Raphael, Dürer, Rubens, Rembrandt and up to Klimt, Schiele and Kokoschka. 1st District, Augustinerstrasse 1; Tel. 534 83-0; only partly open due to renovation work, until further notice.
Heeresgeschichtliche Museum (Military Museum). The most important military history museum in Europe, but also a place of horror documenting the wars of the Habsburgs. 3rd District, Ghegastrasse, Arsenal 18; Tel. 795 61-0; daily except Fridays, 10.00–16.00.
Historisches Museum der Stadt Wien (Historical Museum of the City of Vienna) 4th District, Karlsplatz (next to the Karlskirche) Interesting collections showing the history of the town from the Roman period to the present. Main points: Parts of the 1683 "Turkish booty"; two city models from the 19th century; commemorative rooms to the dramatist Franz Grillparzer and the architect Adolf Loos; a collection of paintings focusing on the late 19th century (Klimt, Schiele). Tel. 505 87 47-0; Tuesdays–Sundays, 9.00–16.30.
Josephinum. The Institute for the History of Medicine of the University of Vienna, housed in a classical building constructed under Joseph II in 1785 as a training centre for military doctors, presents a somewhat bizarre curiosity: as a means of coping with the chronic lack of corpses for students to practice dissection, anatomic wax models were made. The collection of realistically dissected entire human bodies and parts bodies dates from the 18th century, is made of translucent Ukrainian bee wax and is unique in the world. Not for weak nerves! 9th District, Währinger Strasse 25; Tel. 403 21 54; Mondays–Fridays (except public holidays), 9.00–15.00.
Jüdisches Museum (Jewish Museum). Opened in 1993 in the former Eskeles-Nako Palace, a Baroque palace from the 18th century near the Stephansplatz and the Graben. The permanent collection documents the history of the Jews of Vienna and the Holocaust. There are also regular temporary exhibitions. The house also contains a book-shop and the Café Teitelbaum

with international Jewish newspapers. 1st District, Dorotheergasse 11; Tel. 535 04 31-0, daily except Saturdays, 10.00–18.00, Thursdays 10.00–21.00.

KunstHaus Vienna. The private museum of the painter Friedensreich Hundertwasser, entirely in the artist's ecological style. On the first floor there is a permanent display of his works, on the second floor temporary exhibitions of 20th century classics. 3rd District, Untere Weissgerberstrasse 13; Tel. 712 04 91; daily, 10.00–19.00.

Kunsthistorisches Museum (Museum of Fine Arts). The main building of this monumental construction in the "Ringstrasse style" is made up of a number of departments, including the picture gallery. The highlights are works by Rubens, Rembrandt, Titian, Dürer and Velasquez and by Pieter Brueghel the elder – the largest collection of this artist's works in the world; other highlights are Raphael's *Madonna in the Meadow*, the *Art of Painting* by Vermeer van Delft, the magnificent views by the younger Canaletto and much more. 1st District, Maria Theresien Platz/Burgring 5; Tel. 525 24-0; Tuesdays–Sundays, 10.00–18.00, picture gallery also Thursdays, 10.00–21.00.

Kupferstichkabinett der Akademie der bildenden Künste (Copperplate Engraving Cabinet of the Academy of Fine Arts). The focus is on hand-drawings, water-colours and prints. The collection is one of the most important for German drawing of the early 19th century. Also worth mentioning are the 277 Gothic stonemason lodge drawings by the Vienna cathedral master-builder Franz Jäger (the largest collection of medieval building sketches in the world). 1st District, Makartgasse 3; Tel. 581 30 40; Tuesdays–Sundays, 10.00–15.00; visits only by appointment, since there are no permanent exhibitions.

Café in the Museum of Fine Arts.

Museum für Völkerkunde (Ethnological Museum). The world's largest ethnological collections, with pride of place going to an Aztec priest's crown, which Mexican Indios have long been demanding back. The permanent displays include the art of the Aztecs and the collection of James Cook, who circumnavigated the earth. Interesting temporary exhibitions. 1st District, Neue Hofburg (Heldenplatz); Tel. 534 30-0; daily except Tuesdays 10.00–16.00.

Museum moderner Kunst Stiftung Ludwig Wien, 20er Haus (Museum of Modern Art,

Ludwig Vienna Foundation, 20er Haus). Temporary exhibitions of contemporary art are shown in the former pavilion of the World Exhibition (Brussels, 1958) by Karl Schwanzer. The "Garden of sculptures" of the 20er Haus shows sculptures of international Modernism. 3rd District, Schweizer Garten; Tel. 799 69 00, Tuesdays–Sundays, 10.00–18.00.

Museum moderner Kunst Stiftung Ludwig Wien, Palais Lichtenstein (Museum of Modern Art, Ludwig Vienna Foundation, Palais Liechtenstein). In the former summer palace of Prince Liechtenstein, this museum has been established around the "Ludwig collection". The setting contrasts well with the exhibited works of informal art, pop art, op-art, object art and other modern movements. 9th District, Fürstengasse 1; Tel. 317 69 00; Tuesdays–Sundays, 10.00–18.00.

Naturhistorisches Museum (Natural History Museum). Since 1899, the huge imperial collections covering everything from insects to dinosaurs have been housed in the architectural counterpoint of the Kunsthistorisches Museum. Highlights include the 25,000 year old statuette of the *Venus of Willendorf* (prehistoric department), a 117 kg heavy giant topaz and Maria Theresia's glittering Rococo jewel flowers in the collection of precious stones. The collections of insects and meteorites are amongst the most significant in the world. 1st District, Maria Theresien Platz/Burgring 7; Tel. 521 77-0; daily except Tuesdays 9.00–18.00, in winter 1st storey only, 9.00–15.00.

Part of the butterfly collection of the Natural History Museum.

Österreichische Galerie des 19. und 20. Jahrhunderts im Oberen Belvedere (The Austrian Gallery of the 19th and 20th Centuries in the Upper Belvedere). Contains the world's largest public collection of works by Gustav Klimt and Egon Schiele, together with classical works of the late 18th century until the Biedermeier period, as well as the favourite of the period of Promotorism, Hans Makart, and the battle scenes by Anton Romako. 3rd District, Prinz Eugen Strasse 27; Tel. 798 41 58; Tuesdays–Sundays, 10.00–17.00.

Österreichisches Museum für Angewandte Kunst – MAK (Austrian Museum of Applied Arts). The Neo-Renaissance museum building dates back to 1867/71, and soon afterwards the corresponding academy also moved in. The museum was refurbished and re-opened in 1993. The building is architecturally and conceptually the most ambitious museum in Vienna, and the main building on the Ring presents a display of design, craftwork, objects of art and utility objects from eight centuries. The rooms are each devoted to different periods and were designed by famous contemporary artists such as Franz Graf, Donald Judd and Jenny Holzer. In addition there are collections on Art Deco, the Vienna Werkstätte, and 20th century design. Furniture from various periods is also shown. The annex shows temporary displays of contemporary art. Next to the main entrance there is an excellent restaurant designed by the architect Hermann Czech. 3rd District, Stubenring 5; Tel. 711 36-0; Tuesdays–Sundays, 10.00–18.00, Thursdays 10.00–21.00.

Weltliche und Geistliche Schatzkammer (Secular and Ecclesiastical Treasury). The most important collection of symbols of power in the whole world, containing the insignias of the Holy Roman Empire (imperial crown, imperial orb, etc.), the family insignias of the Habsburgs, including the crown of Emperor Rudolf II (around 1600), which from 1804 to 1918 was the crown of the Austrian Empire, as well as the Treasure of Burgundy and the insignias of the Order of the Golden Fleece. Other treasures include a huge antique bowl made of agate, the largest emerald in the world weighing 2800 carat, and the legendary "unicorn", a 243 cm long narwhal tusk, as well as liturgical implements and vestments, and precious relics. 1st District, Hofburg (Swiss wing); Tel. 533 60 46; Wednesdays–Mondays, 10.00–18.00

Mozart Monument in the Burggarten.

Vienna – the World Capital of Music

Vienna's reputation as a city of music dates back to the Middle Ages. Under the Babenbergs, the city was a centre for Minnesänger (troubadours) such as Walther von der Vogelweide, for "Spielleute" (wandering minstrels) and for religious music. The Habsburgs, too, had always been great music-lovers. For instance, Maximilian I founded the Imperial Band in 1498, the centre of Viennese music life until well into the 18th century, attracting musicians from the whole of Europe (the Chapel Boys' Choir was the precursor of the famous Vienna Boys' Choir). In the 17th century, the Catholic Church exploited the musical passion of the Viennese to further the counter-reformation. Above all the Jesuits proved to be excellent strategists in the art of persuasion, using the theatre as a means of propaganda in order to win back the "strayed" Lutheran sheep to the Catholic flock. These "Jesuit dramas" set to music represented an important stimulus for music theatre in Vienna. They were soon joined by a new art form from Italy, opera, as well as masques and pageants from Spain. These influences combined ultimately to create the Baroque opera, which Vienna embraced in all its opulence. The first opera performance at the Vienna Court took place in 1625. But it was only under the first great Baroque sovereign Leopold I (1658–1705), who himself was a highly talented musician and composer, that the Italian opera experienced its heyday. A huge wooden opera house was constructed with three tiers and a stage that allowed all the refinements of Baroque theatre mechanics. Sumptuous open air performances also took place, and festive operas by Italian masters had long been on the programme before Christoph Willibald Gluck, the champion of modern musical theatre, and Mozart were able to achieve the break-through for operatic art north of the Alps.

With Mozart (1756–91), an outstanding personality made his appearance on the stage of Viennese musical history. As early as the age of six, the child prodigy from Salzburg was giving piano concerts (his performance before Maria Theresia is legendary), later becoming director of the Archbishop of Salzburg's orchestra in Salzburg. In 1781 he settled in Vienna, where he created his most famous compositions (including the operas *Il Seraglio*, *The Marriage of Figaro* and *The Magic Flute*) either as a free composer or on court commissions.

Together with Haydn and Beethoven, Mozart forms the great trinity of the "Viennese classic", which finally established Vienna's world reputation as a city of music.

Joseph Haydn (1732–1809) the first Classical genius, became famous far beyond the borders of his home country with his chamber music, symphonies and oratorios. He was particularly respected in England, where the king in person attempted to persuade him to take up permanent residence in London. In any event, in England Haydn might have escaped his macabre posthumous fate. For who knows what Viennese sloppiness was the reason why, eleven years after his death, on the occasion of the transfer of the body from Vienna to Eisenstadt, a gruesome discovery was made: the body had no head. At the time the issue was covered up and a wrong head was placed in the new Eisenstadt grave, until one day the real skull turned up in the Vienna Musikverein and was finally returned to its proper owner.

Concert by the Vienna Concert Quintet in the Sala Terrena of the Deutschordenshaus in Singerstrasse.

In 1810, one year after the death of Haydn, the history of Viennese opera took a major step forward with the founding of the "Imperial and Royal Court Opera Theatre by the Kärntnertor" – just at the beginning of the period in which Viennese music life reached its climax: the Biedermeier. This was the period of the works by Ludwig van Beethoven (1770–1827), the culmination of Viennese Classicism, who had come from Bonn to Vienna to study with Haydn. It was also at this time that Franz Schubert (1797–1828), his contemporary and great admirer, achieved the transition from Classicism to Romanticism. He was the creator of a new type of song in which the piano played a major role, and his art and life were often wrongly seen by the following generation in terms of a sweet Biedermeier cliché.

"Wherever you go you hear music ... Music is the pride of the Viennese and hence practically the most important part of their education", wrote Charles Sealsfield, an exile from Austria, in 1827. Music penetrated all fields of life. Alongside the great masters and splendid performances there were countless amateur quartets, choirs and music-making in the home. Music and singing were also an integral part of the theatre. A top quality instrument industry (pianos, violins and organs) was available, music schools were created and the first music journals made their appearance. With the Gesellschaft der Musikfreunde (Society of the Friends of Music), the Conservatoire, the Male Voice Choir and last but not least the Vienna Philharmonic Orchestra, famous institutions were created that have continued to mark Viennese music life to the present. The passion for opera spread. Popular singers made the typical Viennese song socially acceptable. But above all, this time saw the birth of the Viennese Waltz, which was to take all levels of society by storm. At court and in the suburbs, couples danced in close bodily contact for the first time, to the horror of the guardians of public morals. And Joseph Lanner and Johann Strauss senior conducted their orchestras in three-four time so successfully that dance-halls and entertainment palaces shot up practically overnight. In 1835, Strauss was appointed director of the Court Ball, followed 30 years later by his son Johann junior, Vienna's undisputed "Waltz king", whose *Blue Danube Waltz* (1867) became Austria's unofficial national anthem. Together with his brothers Joseph and Eduard, Johann Strauss junior gave classical maturity to the waltz. Works like *Die Fledermaus* (1873) also ensured world fame for Vienna's operetta, which was experiencing its golden age at the time. Like the waltz, it is a musical genre that vividly embodied the phenomenon of "Viennese music".

Another typically popular musical tradition can trace its roots back to this period: Schrammel music, a type of popular chamber music, a carefree light music of a high artistic quality. The style was founded by the two violinists Johann and Josef Schrammel, who were joined by a guitarist in 1878. A little later they were joined by a B clarinet, whose high, *sprightly* sound quickly caught on amongst the Viennese, but was ultimately replaced by the softer, more emotional sounds of the accordion. The Schrammel Quartet played in bars and wine gardens, and its melodies, including the march *Wien bleibt Wien*, acquired a huge popularity. Today, "Schrammelmusik" has become a generic name. No longer applying to its original creators, the term describes the classical "moaning" old Viennese Heuriger sound, produced by violins, guitar and accordion, a style that nowadays is also performed in concerts (the "Wiener Konzertschrammeln") or enriched with elements of rock ("Neu-wirth Extrem-Schrammeln").

At the turn of the century, Vienna could boast musicians of the very best quality: the Romantic composers Johannes Brahms, Anton Bruckner and Hugo Wolf made Vienna once again the adopted home of three outstanding artists, followed by Gustav Mahler and Richard Strauss, who both directed the new Court Opera House for a time. The new opera building on the Ring had been opened in 1869, and today is one of the best opera houses in the world. At the time, of course, the press, the Imperial Buildings Office and fellow-architects followed the usual Viennese tradition and made a concerted attack on the two architects Sicardsburg and van der Nüll: "As heavy as a digesting elephant" was the reaction to the building. And when it opened with Mozart's opera *Don Giovanni* (initially known as *Don Juan*), its two creators were already dead: Eduard van der Nüll had hanged himself the year before, while his friend August Sicard von Sicardsburg had died shortly thereafter of a broken heart.

But it was not only the builders whose life was made a misery, the directors (and not only then) suffered the same fate. Thus, although the Vienna Opera House became the leading artistic institution of Central Europe under Gustav Mahler (1897–1907), and although Mahler dominated Viennese musical life both as a composer and a conductor, nevertheless he had influential

Monument to the "Waltz King" Johann Strauss in the Stadtpark.

"Swan Lake" at the State Opera House; the ensemble acknowledges the final applause.

opponents in conservative circles and finally capitulated in the face of their virulent campaigns. He submitted his resignation in 1907, despite an open letter from Klimt, Schnitzler, Freud and others, who in vain tried to persuade Mahler to stay.
The letter had also been signed by Arnold Schönberg (1874–1951), himself one of the "disapproved". Influenced by Mahler, Schönberg founded, together with his pupils Alban Berg and Anton Webern, the New Viennese School, whose twelve tone system represented one of the most important breaks in musical history. But at the time, it was not rare for the presentation of his atonal works to end in scandal, such as in the Grosse Musikvereinssaal in 1913, when violent uproar reached such a stage that the room had to be cleared. The operetta composer Oscar Strauss commented dryly: "The slap in the face was probably the most melodious event of the whole evening." Schönberg's successors Franz Schreker, Ernst Krenek and Gottfried von Einem also attracted plenty of public dissatisfaction. Today, they are well established composers. An Ernst Krenek Institute was opened in the Musikverein in 1998 to cultivate the memory of the great master of twelve tone music, and the same year saw the opening of the Vienna Arnold Schönberg Centre. Vienna, which so often resisted any attempts to honour its geniuses, today prefers to present the greatness rather than the turbulence of its past: its unique succession of great composers or the reputation of its teaching institutions and performance venues, its orchestras, archives and instrument makers. The Goldene Saal of the Musikverein, the Bösendorfer piano makers, the Vienna Philharmonic Orchestra and the State Opera are synonymous with sophisticated musical culture. The Vienna Boys' Choir, the Opera Ball and the New Year's Concert are a successful means of worldwide propagation of the joyfulness of the Viennese waltz and operetta.
After 1945, Vienna lost its leading position in the field of contemporary composition. Only since the 1980s has there been a revival in new music – with Friedrich Cerha, Kurt Schwertsik or Otto M. Zykan as pioneers; with stimulating series of events such as *Wien Modern* (in the Konzerthaus). Other musical areas revived more quickly: singer-songwriters and pop singers such as Wolfgang Ambros, Georg Danzer and Falco created Austro-pop, which created a sensation in the 1970s with song texts that at times were in an incomprehensible Viennese dialect. And in the 1980s, another popular sector hit the limelight. Thanks to popular hits such as *Cats and Elisabeth*, Vienna became one of the world's leading cities for musicals.
Similarly, the geniuses of the international jazz scene are regular visitors to Vienna, and not only at the annual Summer Jazz Festival, during which for once very different rhythms can be heard in the State Opera House and the Volkstheater, but also in clubs such as "Jazzland" and "Porgy & Bess". It is here that live performances by national and international stars take place daily. The "Porgy" is partly run by the composer Mathias Rüegg, for over twenty years the bandleader of the world famous Vienna Art Orchestra.

Theatre, Cabaret and Review

Viennese cultural life is based on two mighty elements, music and theatre. These are the highly sensitive core of Viennese cultural activity and are capable of arousing passions in this city perhaps even more than any major political event. Indeed, they themselves have more than occasionally become a political issue, as would be testified by the Opera House directors from Gustav Mahler to Herbert von Karajan or the heads of the National Theatre from Anton Wildgans to Claus Peymann, whose production of Thomas Bernhard's provocative play *"Heldenplatz"* split the nation in 1988. Even those who never go to the theatre cannot escape its influence. Cast-lists, dismissals, world premiers, gossip – everything is taken with deadly seriousness and fills the columns of the daily press. Cultural reports are even a daily part of the TV evening news. The artist is fortunate indeed who can become a celebrated darling of the people against a background of such complex interest. The best stepping stone to cult status is the National Theatre, for many the Olympus of drama in the German-speaking world, for others a stronghold of tradition or even the guarantee of national identity. It is hence no surprise that the winds of emotion blow particularly strongly at this seat of myths and scandals.

As so often, however, it all began in a very "un-Austrian" manner. A decisive stimulus came with the arrival from beyond the Alps in the late Middle Ages of the Commedia del'arte, whose players were particularly welcome at the Habsburg courts. The Italian troupes were the first to acquaint the Viennese public with professional theatre, drama and ensembles, although in an exclusively court setting; for this reason German theatre, which was just developing at the time, followed more closely the example of English troupes of actors who were travelling the continent at the time. It was only in the 18th century that the model of the Commedia del arte had a widespread effect – a development that began above all in Vienna and also left its longest and most clearest traces in the old Viennese popular theatre. "Hanswurst" (Harlequin) and "Kasperl" (Punch) became the most popular stage figures and managed to survive into the theatre literature of the following centuries despite authoritarian reforms and a strict censorship of the coarse impromptu performances. Ferdinand Raimund and Johann

One of the most famous concert halls in the world: the Golden Hall of the Musikverein.

View from the Town Hall to the National Theatre.

Nestroy, and indeed even the great "classicist" Franz Grillparzer, could not escape their influence. Even today every Viennese child knows "Kasperl" from puppet theatre.

And while the populace bent double in laughter at the antics of Harlequin in the Kärntnertor Theater, the precursors of today's National Theatre were also being created. "There must be a spectacle!" sighed Empress Maria Theresia and, with little enthusiasm, founded the "Royal Theatre by the Burg" in the Ballhaus on the Michaelerplatz in 1741. The theatre, in which for the first time nobility and middle class sat together, presented a mixed repertoire: French theatre, Italian Singspiel, opera, ballet and German comedies. In 1776 Emperor Joseph II issued the order to continue the theatre under the name of the "German National Theatre".

In the meantime, the Kärntnertor Theater had been burned down to the ground, thus putting an end to Hanswurst's coarse jollity. The building was reconstructed by the court architect, Nicolaus Pacassi, in 1763 on the same spot, and from then on the now "Imperial Court Theatre by the Kärntnertor" was the venue for serious works. From 1794, the theatre was used exclusively for ballet and opera, thus making the separation that has applied ever since: musical theatre in the Opera House, spoken drama in the National Theatre. As early as 1814 the National Theatre under the direction of Joseph Schreyvogel achieved the first rank amongst German-speaking theatres thanks to its performances of high drama, classical plays and an international repertoire. Alongside these theatres "for those of so-called fine taste", as one contemporary put it, there was a large number of private suburban theatres, such as the small "Theater im Freihaus", which saw the first performance of Mozart's *Magic Flute* under its director Emanuel Schikaneder in 1791. When this closed down, Schikaneder founded the "Imperial and Royal Private Theatre by the Wien" not far away in 1801, which was to become one of the most popular theatres in the city (today the Theater an der Wien, Linke Wienzeile 6). His overladen productions in this huge and sumptuous building unscrupulously exploited the Viennese lust for spectacle. The programme covered every type of stage work, from popular comedies to opera, and the house staged the first performances of both Grillparzer's *Ahnfrau* and Beethoven's only opera *Fidelio*.

In contrast, the Leopoldstätter Theater was dedicated entirely to Viennese popular theatre. Founded in 1781, its creation of the figure of "Kasperl" ensured it a huge popularity. All Vienna spoke of the "Kasperltheater". It was followed by other comic types who populated the romantic and comical popular fairy tales, parodies and local farces. One of the actors of the acclaimed ensemble was Ferdinand Raimund, who had moved from the Josefstädter Theater in 1817. Soon he was also writing for the stage, and became the precursor and at times rival of Nestroy. Raimund (1790–1836) shaped the old Viennese fairy tale and magic plays into something more poetic, full of humour and melancholy, and his plays such as *Der Bauer als Millionär* and *Der Verschwender* formed the basis of a genuine popular theatre. His actual dream had been to write tragedies like his hero Grillparzer, and to have them performed in the National Theatre. That this latter wish would one day be fulfilled never occurred to him during his lifetime.

Johann Nestroy (1801–62) was also one of the most popular comedians and playwrights of his day, initially at the Theater an der Wien and then at the Carltheater (the successor to the Leopoldstädter Theater). Like Raimund, he is regarded as a classical representative of Vienna popular theatre, although far more realistic and critical. His sharp wit, his incessant play on words and his biting satire are timeless, and influenced writers such as Karl Kraus, Bert Brecht and Friedrich Dürrenmatt.

The Carltheater where Nestroy celebrated his triumphs no longer exists today. But another suburban stage of the time, the Theater in der Josephstadt has survived, after a chequered history. Ferdinand Raimund's original stage struggled to keep its head above water. For a long time an acknowledged opera stage that even successfully rivalled the Court Opera, the house survived a number of depressions until finally closing in 1923. This was no obstacle to a new start, and the great man of the theatre, Max Reinhardt (1873–1943), rented the house, had it refurbished and achieved huge successes with a troupe

Closing curtain in the State Opera House.

that amongst others included Fritz Kortner, until his emigration in 1938. In 1929, the famous director founded an actor's seminar in the Schönbrunn Palace Theatre that was intended to train young actors for the Reinhardt stages in Austria and Germany, and is still today Vienna's most renowned training centre for the theatre. The Viennese passion for the theatre continues unabated today. Over-passionate fans may no longer hitch themselves to the cabs of their adored artists in enthusiasm (if only because of the lack of cabs), but they still queue for hours to obtain tickets for first nights. Young people still crowd the cheap standing spaces in accordance with a long tradition, and even those whose obsession is like that of Hans Christian Andersen whenever he visited Vienna, can still go to the theatre every day without ever getting bored. Alongside the Burgtheater (National Theatre), there is also the Akademietheater (the Burg's small stage), the Volkstheater (with a tendency towards modern theatre) and the Theater an der Josephstadt (focus on society plays); the Theater an der Wien and the Raimundtheater are today largely stages for musicals, while the Ronacher presents musicals and variety theatre. In addition there are plenty of interesting medium-sized and small stages, such as the Schauspielhaus (committed avant-garde), Gruppe 80 (focus on Austrian popular theatre), Ensemble Theater (contemporary drama), Drachengasse 2 (women's subjects in the broadest sense), Vienna's English Theatre (often with top-quality guest stars), the International Theatre, Kammerspiele and Kleine Kommödie (boulevard comedies), as well as the venues for the numerous independent groups such as the Theater im Künstlerhaus, Theater-Forum or Theater-Brett. Mention should also be made of the Odeon, the home of the internationally successful mime group "Serapionstheater"; the premises of the former Fruit Exchange, themselves well worth seeing, also stage guest performances of music, theatre and dance. The Erste Wiener Stegreifbühne (previously "Tschauner"), in existence since 1909, may no longer have its old flair but still remains an earthy curiosity in the theatre landscape.

The Serapions-theater now plays in the "Odeon" in the 2nd District.

One particular type of stage art is the Viennese cabaret, that experienced its heyday in the inter-war period. Whether one-act play, revue or one-man show, whether more literary or political, now more aggressive, now less so – a wide range of authors created a cabaret literature full of sharp wit, wise irony and incorrigible local colour for a large number of legendary cabaret stages in the period between the wars. Thus the double act and cabaret reviews developed by Fritz Grünbaum and Karl Farkas determined the style of the "Simpl", a stage that still exists today, despite the loss of its sparkle.

1938 saw the end of the era of cabaret. Criticism and satire were forbidden, exile or deportation was the fate of the many Jewish writers, such as Fritz Grünbaum, who did not survive Dachau. The cultural scene was irredeemably destroyed, a scene that had produced popular idols such as Hans Moser; as a small, grumpy figure with a high-pitched moaning voice, he later became a Viennese institution through his countless films.

Karl Farkas returned in 1946 and continued the "Simpl". Stella Kadmon, whose "Lieber Augustin", opened in 1931, was

The Ronacher, newly renovated, is a venue for variety theatre and musicals.

the first political cabaret stage in Vienna, returned from exile in Palestine in 1947 and in 1948 founded the avant-garde stage "Theater der Courage", which brought Bertolt Brecht to Vienna and survived until 1981. At the same time a new cabaret group formed, whose satirical approach attacked the Vienna of the post-war years with its failure to come to terms with the past. *Brettl vor'm Kopf* was the promising name of the first legendary programme of which every Viennese even today knows at least a couple of titles, songs or quotations. The actor Helmut Qualtinger, the cabaretist Gerhard Bronner and the wicked chansonnier Georg Kreisler are only a few of the names that appeared in this group and who also achieved a reputation through their other works. In the 1970s, a new generation appeared on the stages of the cabaret theatres, in the form of Lukas Resetarits. With an overwhelming political accent to begin with, the programme has now become much broader. From political cabaret to pure entertainment, a varied scene has developed with stars such as Josef Hader and Alfred Dorfer, who also achieved fame beyond the limits of Vienna through their film *Indien*. Countless cabaret stages, mostly connected with restaurants and bars, have developed and are developing, including "Kulisse", "Spectakel", "Orpheum", "Vindobona", "Niedermair", "Vorstadt" and "Metropol", whose programmes are to be found in all the Viennese what's-on magazines and daily newspapers.

Literature

The most important period for literary life in Vienna was the 19th century, which saw a particularly broad development in this field. Alongside Ferdinand Raimund and Johann Nestroy, the consummate touch to the old Viennese popular theatre, this was also the era of Austria's most important dramatist, Franz Grillparzer (1791–1872), the "classic" of Viennese theatre, who in form and language continued the tradition of Schiller and Goethe. He also left behind important works of fiction, a collection of lyrics and religious and literary studies. A civil servant by profession, with the title of Hofrat (Court Councillor), Grillparzer, a typical Viennese, was a victim of the deepest self-doubt and dissatisfaction. Like many contemporaries, he suffered under the ordained intellectual narrowness of his age and from a censorship that imposed its dictatorship on writers more than any other artists. Thus it was only with great difficulty that Grillparzer's *König Ottokars Glück und Ende*, a drama about the history of the Habsburgs, managed to achieve a performance. From then on Grillparzer's only comment on Metternich's police state was a grim "so be it", and subsequently he withdrew himself entirely. The most important writer of fiction of the time was Adalbert Stifter, who lived from 1828 to 1848 in Vienna. Stifter, who was also a painter, has long been misinterpreted as the master of the Biedermeier idyll, with his gentle feeling for the small, the quiet and the inconspicuous; today he is regarded as one of the great prose writers of the German language and probably its greatest (literary) painter of landscapes. The first protests against the appalling social conditions can be found in the realistic tales and novels of Marie Ebner-Eschenbach, the most famous female Austrian writer of the 19th century. This sensitive aristocrat moved from Moravia to Vienna in 1863, living and working there until her death in 1916.

Peter Altenberg on Stephansplatz, surrounded by three "Graben-Nymphen" (prostitutes). Water-coloured drawing by Remigius Geyling (1902).

It was precisely at this time that literary Vienna experienced an unprecedented climax. During the period of promotorism, Vienna was a hive of activity. Writers, artist and intellectuals gathered in the sparkling salons such as those of Berta Zuckerkandl and Franziska von Wertheimstein. The number of coffee-houses multiplied, giving rise to a unique literary genre: the Vienna coffee-house literature. One of its origins was the Griensteidl Café on the Michaelerplatz, where the *Young Vienna* circle of writers met. This group included Hermann Bahr, Hugo von Hofmannsthal, Peter Altenberg, Arthur Schnitzler and many others, and sought for new forms of literary expression, to the derision of Karl Kraus, who thought little of these "coffee-house decadent modernists".

Yet Kraus (1874–1936) himself was a regular visitor to the coffee-house, first of all the Griensteidl and then the Café Central, but saw himself in literary terms more as an outsider. He founded and ran his own journal, the Fackel, the mouthpiece for his own cultural criticism. As a protest against the madness of the war, he wrote *Die letzten Tage der Menschheit* (The Last Days of Mankind) (1918/19), an extensive collage of texts; it was his main dramatic work, one which, as he said, he had written for a "theatre on Mars", he himself imagining it to be unperformable. At the same time this critic of language and the age wrote unerring essays, satires, aphorisms and poems.

The Café Griensteidl (water-colour by R. Völkl, 1896) was the meeting point of Viennese literary society around 1900.

"What is a coffee-house writer? A person who has the time to sit in the coffee-house and think about what the others are not experiencing outside." This definition originates from Vienna's king of witticisms, Anton Kuh (1890–1941) a talented bohemian and scrounger like many of his coffee-house friends, Kuh survived on his biting witticisms, his humorous anecdotes and brilliant analyses, which he would produce impromptu on any occasion. He died in exile in New York in 1941.

His contemporary Arthur Schnitzler (1862–1931), whose famous play *Der Reigen* presented a genre painting of fin-de-siècle society, was one of the most performed authors in the period before 1914. This despite the fact that the unconventional play initially triggered a violent scandal and indeed was occasionally banned until it became a stage success and – much later – was also filmed. Today, Schnitzler is regarded as one of the most important Austrian dramatists, and his plays caught the mood of Vienna's middle class at the turn of the century in such a sensitive way that Sigmund Freud had no choice but to write in an admiring letter to the author: "For many years I have been aware of the wide-reaching agreement between your and my interpretation of many a psychological and erotic problem ...". Stefan Zweig (1881–1942), whose novels and short stories, including the *Schachnovelle*, were a hit world-wide, was also indebted to Viennese Impressionism, Symbolism and psychoanalysis. In the last years of the monarchy, a new literary movement began to make its appearance: Expressionism, whose most important exponents were the poet Georg Trakl, the writer Franz

Theodor Csokor and the poetry-writing pain-ters Alfred Kubin and Oskar Kokoschka.
In the inter-war period, a number of the greatest German-speaking novelists were active in Vienna, novelists whose importance for Austrian literature cannot be overestimated: Robert Musil (1880–1942), whose monumental fragment *Der Mann ohne Eigenschaften* (The Man without Qualities) presents a multi-layered picture of the decline of "Kakania", the name he gave to the Habsburg monarchy; Hermann Broch (1886–1951), who like Musil attempted to record the downfall of an era with scientific preciseness, or Joseph Roth (1894–1939), who dealt not only with the end of the monarchy (in, amongst other works *Radetzkymarsch*), but also with the decline of eastern Jewry.
Finally Heimito von Doderer (1896–1966), with his famous novel *Die Strudlhofstiege*, is the most representative writer of post-war Vienna, which otherwise still bore the marks of the intellectual "cleansing" of the Third Reich. The pre-war traditions were taken up stylistically by only a few, such as Fritz Hochwälder (1911–86) or Alexander Lernet-Holenia (1897–1976). Others such as Friederike Mayröcker and Ernst Jandl, no doubt the most famous Viennese poet, and the legendary *Viennese Group* around H. C. Artmann, pursued the avant-garde path by experimenting with language in text montages, sound poems and dialect texts – works which, like Ingeborg Bachmann's novel *Malina*, were created in a relationship of tension to Vienna. At that time, Bachmann was part of the literary circle that was based in the Café Raimund, focusing on the writer Hans Weigl, who encouraged young literary talents. Like Weigl, his colleague Friedrich Torberg (1908–79) had also returned from exile after the war. Torberg saw himself as a critic and journalist in the tradition of Karl Kraus, and founded the cultural journal *Forum*, which campaigned vehemently

against Bert Brecht (Brecht was boycotted for political reasons in Vienna until 1959). Torberg also wrote novels (including *Der Schüler Gerber*) and translated Ephraim Kishon, making him popular in the German speaking world.
In the 1970s, literary life flourished on the back of political commitment and a critical examination of the city. Newcomers at the time, such as Elfriede Jelinek, Peter Turrini

or Thomas Bernhard, are today amongst the most important and most performed authors of the German-speaking world; they were followed in the 1980s by Christoph Ransmeier, who achieved international reputation with his novel *Die letzte Welt*. Today there is a lively multi-faceted literary scene with authors well known beyond Austria's borders alongside "local heroes". The infrastructure, too, is developing, with journals, publishing houses, bookstores, cafés and centres such as the "Literary Quarter in the Alte Schmiede" or the "Literature House" ensuring a broad impact through readings and events. And of course there are still the coffee-houses such as the Prückel, the Café Museum or the Sperl that continue to have their regular literary visitors.

Café in the Museum of Applied Art (MAK).

International Vienna

Vienna has always been a city of immigration, with the Habsburg capital acting like a magnet for countless numbers hoping for work, education and a career. "It was here that all the rivers of European culture came together", wrote the Austrian writer Stefan Zweig in his autobiography *Die Welt von gestern*. "The real genius of this city of music was to dissolve all the contrasts harmoniously into something new and unique, into the Austrian, into the Viennese." Countless giants of politics, science, art and culture, without whose achievements the historical and cultural attainments of this country could never have happened, were not from Vienna nor even from Austria – which should not strike us as particularly unusual given all the coming and going at this heart of power in Central Europe. It is only today that the extent and naturalness of the multicultural influences in this city are regarded as rather astonishing, and it is quite characteristic of this once pluralistic Vienna that for instance the Roman Pietro Metastasio, court poet in Vienna from 1729, managed to live here for over fifty years without any difficulties and yet was unable to speak a single word of German. If it was the Italians from the field of art and culture who were a permanent fixture of the Viennese Baroque era, in the 19th century it was above all the inflow of labour from all the corners of the multi-ethnic state that dominated the colourful streets of the city. Its rapid growth after the bastions were razed attracted a flood of "guest-workers" hoping to find work in the new industries or the many construction projects. A large number were Czechs, many of whom settled in the Favoriten district of Vienna (a relic of this is the "Bohemian Prater", an entertainment park on the Laaerberg still worth visiting today); they were accompanied by Hungarians, Italians, Jews, Poles and many other "visitors" from all parts of the monarchy, indeed from the whole of Europe. Around 1910, almost one-third of the inhabitants of Vienna came from areas outside Modern Austria. At the time, the city of two million inhabitants was the second largest Czech and Jewish city in Europe (with a population only marginally greater than today). From the Bohemian bricklayers to the Bohemian cook or the house-maid from the Bukovina in the fine middle-class Viennese households – the economic dynamism of the end of the century would have been unthinkable without the immigrants. But they not only spurred on the economic, intellectual and cultural life of the country, they also and above all made their mark on everyday life. The Viennese dialect has taken up countless expressions that derive from the languages of other peoples. Examples are: "potschert" (clumsy), from the Hungarian *bocs* – a young bear, while the "Strizzi" (small crook, pimp) comes from the Czech *strye*, uncle; and one of the many contributions from Yiddish is the word "Zores" (from *zorah*, worries). Viennese cuisine is composed of influences from throughout the monarchy, from Bohemian pastries and Italian ice-cream to Hungarian goulash and Serbian Reisfleisch. Indeed even the utterly typical Wienerschnitzel is by no means from Vienna, as one might assume, but from Italy, imported by a Milanese cook who introduced it to the court of Maria Theresia in the 18th century. The Vienna telephone directory, too, with its long lists of tongue-twisting or by now normal-sounding Slav or Hungarian names, is a reminder of this colourful and creative, but also highly explosive Viennese concoction. For the melting pot of Vienna, with its mixture of languages, cultures and identities, was also a powder keg. The

Service in the synagogue in the Seitenstettengasse.

many contrasts might have been dissolved more or less harmoniously at a cultural level, but in everyday life and in politics the situation was different. Anti-Semitism and resentment flourished. Official Vienna saw itself by no means as a multi-national city. Nor was it any different throughout the rest of the monarchy. The many peoples did not live alongside each other in peace and equality, and instead many minorities suffered serious disadvantages. Thus German was the language of officialdom, even in the furthest corners of Galizia. And the slightest adjustment of power gave rise to riots and protests. The colourful bouquet of nationalities concealed a time-bomb, but the already weak monarchy studiously ignored its ticking. Finally it was the unsolved nationality question that played a part in the collapse in the huge multi-ethnic state of Austro-Hungary.

Thus both then and today there is no avoiding conflict. The "golden Viennese heart" can cool down amazingly quickly if it wants to. And it is indeed a strange phenomenon that many of the Viennese, practically all of whom reflect the Danube's multicultural mixture in their family trees, immediately abandon pluralism as soon as it gets uncomfortable in any way – with barbarous consequences, as history has shown.

Nevertheless, the patchwork of colourful cultures continues unceasingly to spread itself out over Vienna. Thus in the 1960s, the beginnings of the economic boom lead to a new mass inflow of guest-workers, mainly labourers from the then Yugoslavia and from Turkey, who found work in factories, on building sites and in restaurant kitchens, as cleaning staff or caretakers, settling in the old working districts of Vienna beyond the Gürtel. They made and continued to make their mark on the areas surrounding the markets, whose revival is largely due to their activity. The Naschmarkt, the Brunnenmarkt, the Karmelitermarkt or the Viktor-Adler-Markt today present a much more varied face than before. Turkish grocers fill a gap in local supplies with their food stores "round the corner". Immigrants from the former Soviet Union, from Poland or Bulgaria have turned the Mexikoplatz near the Danube into a widely known market place for all kinds of cheap goods, its countless brightly coloured shops bringing a touch of Eastern Europe into Vienna. Or again, the newspaper vendors on the streets of the city almost all come from Arabian countries. The 1.8 million inhabitant metropolis is home to roughly 270,000 immigrants, and the problems and friction have not become less over the years – merely different.

In 1991, the Viennese surprisingly voted in a referendum against holding the World Exhibition in Vienna, a reaction that was seen by many as reflecting an inclination towards isolation and an act of xenophobia. Since then, Austria has joined the European Union. The country has opened up, but at the same time closed its borders to immigrants from eastern and south-eastern Europe. On the other hand, the flow of visitors from the countries of the EU and the Far East is increasing, and the city is trying to establish a cosmopolitan flair based not least on Vienna's role as a popular tourist destination, as an international congress city and as the headquarters of numerous United Nations' organisations. Seen thus, Vienna is once again becoming a colourful international city, not without problems by any means, but with years of experience to learn from.

The Islamic centre on the Danube includes two mosques.

The coffee-house

Over 300 years old and surrounded by myths for almost 100 years, the coffee-house is a Viennese institution of the first order, the focus of countless anecdotes and rumours. The very beginning is wreathed in legend: After the siege of Vienna in 1683, the Turks are alleged to have left sacks of an inconspicuous greyish green bean behind, that were picked up by a certain Kolschitzky; as a reward for his useful scouting services, he was said to have been made the first Viennese coffee-house owner. So much for one of Vienna's most popular rumours. For it was not the Polish spy Kolschitzky but an Armenian merchant named Deodato who is known to have been granted the first coffee-serving privilege, and that in 1685. And Armenian merchants played a leading role in the coffee shop trade of the city for many a year. Nor is it simply a rumour that this trade rapidly became a success with the (initially exclusively male) public. The pleasures of coffee were supplemented by further entertainments in the 18th century: billiards and chess, or newspapers. And in the 19th century, the coffee-house became one of the main focuses of social life, with luxurious furnishings in the city, or cheaper, although no less ostentatious, in the suburbs. It was here that the regular guest drank "his" coffee, read "his" newspaper, played, meditated or made conversation. It was (and is) also possible to eat in the coffee-house. And it was in the concert cafés of the Biedermeier period that the waltz kings gave their performances. Finally, the turn of the century saw the climax proper of the Viennese coffee-house culture. Side by side, at least so it is rumoured, the brilliant minds sat around the marble tables, in front of them a "Mocca" or an "Einspänner", above them the thick clouds of cigar smoke, with a note-book

and a newspaper always within reach, and for anyone who wished to listen there was the staccato beat of their brilliant wordplay. Their home was possibly simply a cold room, if at all, for lack of money. So goes the legend, so it is told in countless anecdotes, and so also it might have been, in the Café Griensteidl, Central or in the Herrenhof. "The talents sit so closely round a table in the coffee-house that they hinder each other in their development",

mocked Karl Kraus, who must have known, for he too sat there alongside Schnitzler, Freud or Hofmannsthal, Loos, Klimt or Schiele, the still unknown operetta composer Franz Lehar and an even less known Mr. Bronstein, alias Leo Trotsky. And the writer Peter Altenberg simply gave his address as "Vienna 1, Café Central". It was then that the coffee-house finally became an institution, for some indeed a "world philosophy". And for many, despite the decline in coffee-houses and the reduced leisure time, it is thus that it has remained. There are still 500 coffee-houses in the whole of Vienna, and for all of them it is still true what Alfred Polgar once said about the Café Central: "The actual delights of this wonderful coffee-house can only be shared by those who want nothing other than to be there. A lack of purpose sanctifies the sojourn."

The café Sacher serves the genuine Sachertorte, but the recipe remains a secret of the house.

Right:
Café Schopenhauer in the 18th District.

Opposite:
Demel's Imperial Court Confectioner's.

A brief course in coffee

Simply order a cup of coffee in a coffee-house and at best you'll encounter an indulgent smile. To enable you to give the right name to Viennese coffee, here is a selection of the most important types.

Grosser/kleiner Schwarzer: A large/small cup of espresso coffee

Grosser/kleiner Brauner: Espresso with a dash of milk

Melange: A small espresso with plenty of milk, some often with a head of whipped cream. Variants of the Melange are, depending on the amount of milk, the "Schale Braun" or the "Schale Gold".

Verlängerter: Diluted with water

Einspänner: Black coffee served in a glass with a portion of whipped cream on top. The name comes from the Viennese fiacre drivers that used to wait in front of the cafés for their customers, holding the reins in one hand and a glass mug of coffee in the other. As a result of the shortage of fodder after the First World War, the cabs were only drawn by one horse – the Einspänner (one-horse cab).

Kapuziner: With a dash of cream.

Eiskaffee: Cold espresso, vanilla ice-cream and whipped cream.

Maz(z)agran: Cold coffee with fragments of ice and a dash of rum.

Turkish coffee: Is served in a copper can, boiling hot and pre-sweetened.

Every order is served with a glass of water – drunk after the coffee, it helps against excess acid in the stomach! More water is always supplied and so you can sit for hours over a small coffee and read the international press.

DEMEL

The Heurige

The Viennese are only too happy to drink, and it is not only with coffee that they have a close relationship but also, and above all, with the juice of the grape. For this reason the cornerstones of Vienna mythology include not only the coffee-house but also the airy venues of tipsiness on the edges of Vienna, the so called Heurige (wine taverns; literally "this year"). These take their name from the young wine from the last harvest that is drawn from the barrel in spring and served directly by the vintner in the Buschenschenken (wine tavern; the difference will shortly be explained). Until 11th November (St. Martin's day), the wine is known as "Heuriger", and afterwards as "old" wine. Wherever a bunch of pine branches hangs from a pole above the gate, you can be sure of a genuine Heuriger – unlike the many copies that have sprung up. The bush implies that the house is open and that only the vintner's own wine is available (a "Buschenschenke", a tavern with a bush). "Ausg'steckt is" (the bush is out) is also the title of one of the many Heurige songs whose preferred subjects (how could it be otherwise?) are wine, Vienna, the intoxication that drowns all sorrows and death itself. More sentimental and grumbling than cheerful or boisterous, they are traditionally accompanied by a violin, an accordion and a guitar.

Heuriger in Oberlaa.

This melancholy charm is best found in the quiet taverns hidden away in the vineyards. In contrast, the large sophisticated Heurige are no longer as original and in fact usually no longer entitled to "put out the bush", i.e. they sell more than their own wine, and they are also subject to the other commercial regulations; at the same time, it is here that one is more likely to hear Heurige songs. In the vineyards, cellars, courtyards and gardens around Vienna, the seating is rustic at the long wooden tables, food is from a copious buffet (self service!), the white wine is drunk from glass mugs, and conversation is with people you've never met before – for the Heurige is a place consecrated to conviviality. For teetotallers there is Most (unfermented grape juice), for connoisseurs Sturm (grape juice that is a few days old and has already started to ferment – caution, risk of diarrhoea!). But remember, no beer. In the genuine old Heurige it is acceptable even today to bring along your own food.

The fact that Vienna is surrounded by vineyards producing excellent – largely white – wine is possibly due to the Celts and certainly to the Romans, who brought their types of vine and cultivation methods to the Danube. There were extensive vineyards in and around Vienna as early as the late middle ages. In 1784 it was decreed that the wine producers were entitled to sell or serve the wine from their own vineyards themselves – the origin of the Heurige. For a time, the harvest yield was so great that imperial decrees not only banned the planting of new vineyards but even ordered sour wine to be used to mix the mortar for the Stephansdom. The Viennese drank up to 120 litres of wine per person and year. And this despite the fact that at times women were banned from entering the Buschenschenken. One traveller wrote about the then village of Neulerchenfeld: "The largest tavern of the Holy Roman Empire where around 16,000 people seek relaxation at any time on a single sunny Sunday."

Thus the visit to the Heurige has a long tradition in Vienna. It is still best in summer, when you can sit outdoors until late into the night with a view of sparkling Vienna from the top end of a vineyard (don't forget an anti-insect spray!). It is also romantic in autumn when the colours of the forests and vineyards around Vienna glow as you drink the fresh Most or Sturm

Vienna is the only metropolis with vineyards within the city limits – here on the Wilhelminenberg.

in the autumn sunshine. Many Heurige are now also open in winter, and you can forget the cold world outside over a glass of Glühwein (hot mulled wine) in a wood-panelled parlour, whether in Grinzing, Sievering, Nussdorf, Heiligenstadt or Neustift am Walde. For a more racy atmosphere you can go to Ottakring or across the Danube, to Strebersdorf or Stammersdorf with their old alleys of cellars, They are further away, but make up by being cheaper, serving a sharper wine and with a genuine atmosphere. Outside Vienna and to the south, there is Perchtoldsdorf and, along with Grinzing no doubt the most famous Heurige village, Gumpoldskirchen (where in the Middle Ages the Pope bought his wine), as well as Guntrams-dorf, Pfaffstätten, Bad Vöslau and Baden.

The Viennese Beisl

The "Beisl" is another special feature that has much to do with the pleasure that the Viennese take in drinking as well as eating. A Beisl is to Vienna what the Bistro is to Paris, the pub to London and the osteria to Rome – a cosy familiar refuge where you don't have to be a regular to recharge your batteries, let off steam, gossip and philosophise. The main components are Viennese cooking, the bar where wine and beer are served to create the right mood, reasonable prices and rather rustic furniture. There is neither a ban on smoking nor any hustle and bustle.
The word "Beisl" derives from Yiddish, via the local thieves' Latin, and actually means "beer joint, dive". But the Beisl is not a place of ill repute, in its original

form it is quite simply popular. Voices are louder than in the coffee-house, the interest is more on physical than intellectual pleasures, and the jokes are mostly some what less sharp-witted. Nevertheless, it can also be said of the common man's second living room that one is "not at home and yet still not in the fresh air." For a true

The famous Tafelspitz (in the Plachutta Restaurant).

Beisl regular always remains in the tap room, even if there is a romantic courtyard or shady guest garden outside.

The Schanigarten (guest garden) is named after the popular Christian name Johann (John), reduced in Viennese to "Schani" (based on the French "Jean"), and is also the synonym for "assistant" or "untrained

The equally famous Wienerschnitzel (in the "Zu den 2 Lieserln" Beisl).

waiter". It was this Schani who had to carry the tables and chairs into the narrow garden in the summer, and to separate them from the street with a wooden fence or tubs of plants. "Schani, take the garden out!" was the call. But careful, it is still not a proper garden.

The Viennese preference for "their" Beisl dates back at least to the time of industrialisation, when everyone was flooding into the factories and building sites of the imperial capital. Accommodation was scarce in the suburbs and villages around the city, and it was not rare for a bed to be used in three shifts, because not everyone could afford one of his own. For this reason, one "lived" in the local Beisl, keeping warm, chatting and drinking. After all, everyone else there was in the same boat.

Seen historically, the Beisl had always been left to itself, until suddenly it was discovered by the "scene" in the 1980s. Chefs invented the new Viennese cuisine, much lighter and digestible, as well as more imaginative than the old one. New establishments arose as sophisticated off-shoots of the once generally proletarian institution, and this revival also included a renaissance of those that already existed. Today, the Beisl with its Viennese cuisine, its more or less excellent wines and well cared for beer is one of the important elements of culinary Vienna. Nevertheless, it is not a restaurant where you eat, drink and move on again. A Viennese Beisl is more, much more.

Viennese cuisine

The success of Viennese cuisine lies in the variety of its constituents: South German, Bohemian, Hungarian, Italian and Balkan influences from the former multi ethnic state have for centuries combined with the cooking traditions of the Alpine regions to produce the wide diversity of dishes that can be enjoyed in Vienna today. The menu with its wealth of dialect expressions is neither light nor low in calories. Meat, fish and offal are all too often given a coating of egg and breadcrumbs and then fried, while the classics without this treatment include beef of all kinds, which plays a particularly important and varied role in Viennese cuisine, and roast pork, accompanied by garnishes such as rice, potatoes, pasta or dumplings as well as a salad

The head cook and his assistants enjoy their meal in the "Schnattl" in the Josefstadt.

(which in Austria is served at the same time as the main course); nor is the classic beef soup served as a starter exactly fat-free, while vast quantities of sugar are used for the rich sweets and cakes served as dessert. Fish and poultry are on practically every menu, and from October to November there is a focus on game with excellent game dishes. Nowadays, vegetarian dishes are also available practically everywhere. And indeed, a new creative style in cooking has firmly established itself. While retaining the inclination towards local tradition, classical Viennese dishes are refined and prepared in a lighter way.

There are also two typically Viennese times for meals between meals: the mid-morning snack (Gabelfrühstück) – most traditionally a small goulash and beer in a tavern or as a roll with a filling of Leberkäs or sausage eaten as you go – and the afternoon snack, classically consisting of coffee and cake or roll. Thus with breakfast, lunch and dinner this means as a rule five diet-free meals which many a heavyweight Viennese will still consume every day with pleasure and without regret. It's hardly surprising that after many of these meals a glass of rowanberry or fruit schnapps is needed to encourage digestion. Meals are mainly accompanied by non-alcoholic drinks, wine or beer. Vienna is extremely well-blessed with eating places of all kinds, qualities, price categories and nationalities. A great advantage of Viennese establishments is that, with the exception of the fine restaurants, you don't necessarily have to eat. It very often happens that at one table one person eats a full three-course meal, another just a soup, two share a dessert and the rest of the group simply have something to drink. This tradition encourages conviviality, and you don't have to decide in advance whether you are going to eat together or just have a beer.

Culinary lexicon

In general, the names are often misleading and should not always be taken literally. Thus Leberkäse (liver cheese) has nothing to do either with liver or with cheese, and the Lungenbraten has nothing to do with lungs. This is compounded by the fact that the Viennese cling ardently to expressions such as "Paradeiser", "Schwammerl" or "Erdapfel" as a symbol of local patriotism.

Backerbsen: Pea-shaped addition to soup made of thick batter.
Backhendl: Chicken fried in breadcrumbs
Beinfleisch: Beef with an edge of fat cooked on the bone
Beuschl: Mince made of calves' lights (lungs), heart and spleen
Buchtel: Small yeast buns usually filled with Powidl (dark plum jam)
Butterschnitzel: Calf meat-cakes.
Erdapfel: Potatoes
Faschiertes: Mince
Fleischlaberl: Meat-cakes
Fisolen: French beans
Fogosch: Pike/perch
Frankfurter: Wiener sausages
Fritatten: Pancake cut into strips and used as an addition to soup
Gebackener Fisch: Fish fried in breadcrumbs.
Germknödel: Yeast dumplings filled with Powidl (dark plum jam)
Geselchtes: Smoked pork
Grammeln: Crispy bits of crackling
Grüner Salat (Häuptelsalat): Lettuce
Guglhupf: Very typical yeast cake
Heurige: New potatoes
Kaiserfleisch: Smoked belly of pork
Kaiserschmarren: Pancakes with raisins cooked in sugar and butter and chopped up.
Kalbsvögerl: Shin veal off the bone
Karfiol: Cauliflower
Knödel: Dumpling
Kohlsprossen: Sprouts

Kren: Horseradish
Krenfleisch: Belly of pork cooked with the rind, sprinkled with horseradish and served with root vegetables.
Kukuruz: Maize
Leberkäse: Type of meat loaf.
Liptauer: Cream cheese made of butter, sheep's cheese, paprika powder and other spices.
Lungenbraten: Fine fillet of beef or pork.
Marille: Apricot
Nockerln: Small dumplings made of egg dough
Palatschinke: Sweet pancakes, usually filled with apricot jam, chocolate or curd cheese.

Vienna's No. 1 gourmet temple: the "Steirereck".

Paniert: Dipped into flower, egg and breadcrumbs and fried
Paradeiser: Tomatoes
Powidl: Very thick plum jam cooked without sugar.
Rostbraten: Steak (not roast beef, as the name might suggest)
Sachertorte: The most famous chocolate cake in the world, filled with apricot jam.
Schlagobers: Sweet whipped cream
Schwammerl: Mushrooms
Semmel, Weckerl: Rolls
Stelze: Knuckle of pork.
Strudel: Speciality made of wafer-thin pulled-out dough filled with curds, apples, nuts, poppy seed or meat.
Tafelspitz: Fine boiled beef served with apple and horseradish or dill sauce; a classic of Viennese cuisine
Topfen: Curd cheese
Vogerlsalat: Lambs' lettuce
Wiener Schnitzel: In the famous original version, veal fried in breadcrumbs served with parsley potatoes. Cheaper, and more common, is the pork schnitzel.
Zwetschke: Plum

The Würstelstand

The Würstelstand (sausage stand) is another culinary institution. Located at numerous corners and squares in the city, they supply passers-by with hot Leberkäs or a pair of Frankfurter (known throughout the rest of the world as "Wiener"), Burenwurst, Klobasse, Waldviertler, Käsekrainer and many more sausages served with mustard – sweet or hot –, a gherkin, pepperoni and lashings of Viennese charm. Particularly in the night and on Sundays, when all other places are closed, a "Hasse" (Burenwurst, literally "Heisse" – hot) or even a hot-dog will keep hunger at bay. No matter how cold the wind blows, no matter how uninviting the night, there will always by a hungry and thirsty crowd of mixed age, sex and social origin in front of the illuminated sliding windows of the Würstelstand. The Würstelstand is one of the most egalitarian places in Vienna, where the building site worker stands side by side with the grey suits, the tramp alongside the yuppie, more or less

Würstelstand on the Naschmarkt.

peacefully at one through the intake of the non-vegetarian delights. Older than any fast food establishment in the city, many of the roughly 300 sausage stands have achieved a fame of their own, as for example the "little Sacher" diagonally opposite the great luxury hotel, just by the Opera House, or the stand on the Hohen Markt, with its often long queues of night owls.

The Fiacre

Like the gondola trip in Venice, a tour of the city in the fiacre is part of the classic visit to Vienna. The tradition dates back over 300 years, the term fiacre referring both to the two-horse carriage and to its coachman (since 1984 also coachwoman). It was in 1693 that the first license was issued in Vien-

na for a fiacre, the name deriving from the rue de Saint Fiacre in Paris, where such hire carriages had already been in existence for a long time. By 1790, there were approximately 700 fiacres on the streets of Vienna, with over a thousand during their heyday from 1860 to 1908. The Carnival Ball of the Fiacres was one of the most famous balls in the city in the 19th century. The coachmen were often well known as singers and whistlers, and who were immortalised in countless anecdotes, books, pictures and songs. The history of this legendary trade is the subject of a small Fiacre Museum (17th District, Veronikagasse 12). Today there are roughly 50 fiacres in Vienna, all in historical get-up, with stands at Stephansplatz, Heldenplatz and Albertinaplatz.

View of the Parliament from Ringstrasse.

Vienna remains Vienna

The clichés about the Viennese fill volumes. They speak of the "golden Viennese heart", of Viennese good naturedness, affability and a tendency to dawdle, of carefreeness and the desire for death, of Viennese "Schmäh" (a special kind of charm) of course, and of the charm of the Viennese women, above all of which hangs a sky full of violins ... "This reputation of a city lulled in the happiness of music and dance,

Wine-tasting in one of the Stammersdorf cellars.

of harmless, slightly slovenly, not very active, not very diligent but good and dear people, has survived outside Vienna. But anyone condemned to live here wouldn't understand it", wrote Hermann Bahr in anger in his book *Wien*, and then turned to the other side of the coin: the self-contempt, opportunism and victim attitude of the Viennese. And he came to the conclusion: "The Viennese is someone who is very unhappy with himself, who hates the Viennese but who cannot live without the Viennese, who despises himself but is moved to tears about himself, who's forever cursing but wants to be forever praised, who feels miserable but at ease in his misery, who's always complaining, always threatening, but puts up with everything except the help of others – this he resists. That is the Viennese." This bitter character study from the beginning of our century has been given countless variations by the Viennese and immigrants. Perhaps the statements are too general, the undertones too dark, but no one can say they are wrong. At most, they are incomplete.

Of course Vienna is a city like any other, where people live, work, pay taxes, play football on Sundays and watch television in the evening. The infrastructure works, even extremely well. As far as crime is concerned, it is one of the safest cities in the world. To this must be added its extraordinarily compact dimensions and a greenbelt with numerous opportunities for excursions and relaxation directly at the front door. The majority is Catholic. The quality of life is high and the Viennese enjoy what their city has to offer. So are they hedonists after all? Are they really as convivial as the songs suggest? Well, it is true that time goes a little slower in Vienna than elsewhere, although here too hustle and bustle is on the increase. Everything is a little more hesitant, more unclear, the way people deal with each other more wishy washy. And certainly the following dialogue could only take place in Vienna: A to B: "Well I must say, you are dreadful." – B (indignant): "But how can you say such a thing?" – C (appeasing): "Calm down. When someone says dreadful they don't mean dreadful."

The Vienna of the long civil service tradition, in which lobbying and tactics were always more important than open conflict, where people prefer to be angry than to state their opinion – this Vienna really exists with all its intrigues, nepotism and etiquette. Titles, balls, funerals; they all exist. Even the Viennese "Schmäh", that "charming sounding expression of spitefulness", in which a single joke can reveal all the enigma and ambivalence of the Viennese, really exists.

And the Viennese strange relationship with death? This remarkable mixture of joie de vivre and the cult of death? It is indeed remarkable how the Viennese love their cemeteries, celebrating funerals, singing of death in countless songs – there is even a funeral museum. Vienna – that "faithful grave by the Danube" as Alfred Polgar once called it. Or is it rather the "land of melancholy", as the writer Jakov Lind felt? It is not by accident that nowhere else in the world has the soul of mankind been more closely examined than in the city of Schnitzler and Freud – and nowhere else have the people wanted to know so little about it. Hypocrisy and obscurity are always preferred and, if necessary, spitefulness. "Sometimes I don't know whether I am a human or a Viennese" said Helmut Qualtinger once, one of the many who suffered from this city. Alfred Polgar put it more sharply. This writer who had remained in exile after the Second World War, came to visit his colleague Friedrich Torberg in Vienna to bring him an article. When Torberg asked how his visitor liked it in Vienna, he answered: "My opinion of this city is devastating. Vienna remains Vienna."

To prevent any misunderstanding, it is by no means the case that this city is dominated entirely by bitterness, resignation and a yearning for death. The city has quite a rebellious and even revolutionary tradition. And alongside the Lodenmantel overcoats and the nasal Schönbrunn German, the symbols of the old Austrian upper-middle class, alongside the lower-middle-class allotments and the Austro-Marxist worker cult, Vienna has always also been the city of masters of the art of living, popular original characters, outsiders, agitators, scroungers, debaters, idlers and bohemians. And it has remained so until the present – a Viennese mixture of characters, mentalities, states of mind and origins. Vienna remains Vienna. Perhaps that is more than just, as Karl Kraus put it, "the most dreadful of all threats".

The grave of honour of the furniture manufacturer Michael Thonet at the Central Cemetery.

Strolls

The Historic Inner City

The boulevards

Kärntner Strasse is one of Vienna's central streets, leading directly from the Opera House to Stephansplatz. First of all it brings a view of the legendary *Hotel Sacher*. The city's hotel-cum-legend was founded in 1876 by Eduard Sacher, the son of a cook and coffee-house owner. He had previously been in Metternich's service, and it was for him that he devised the *Sachertorte*, the cake that was subsequently to become so famous. The original recipe is still the best-guarded secret of the hotel. Anna Sacher, Eduard's resolute, cigar smoking widow, finally secured the world-wide reputation of this hotel in the years following 1892, making it a Viennese institution in its own right. It was here that the aristocracy took their pleasures with the "sweet Viennese girls" from the Imperial Opera Ballet in the discrete séparées, and it was here that the international high society from around the globe resided. Crowned heads, famous personalities and the wealthy – they all left a permanent testimony to their stay by signing Anna Sacher's legendary damask table cloth, still kept alongside other historical treasures. The Sacher was nicknamed "Hotel World History", a reputation based in particular on the still-surviving marble hall with its illustrious banquets and conferences. And it is not all that long ago that John Lennon and Yoko Ono created a sensation by holding a press conference naked in their hotel bed in the name of peace. Today, guests and tourists flood into the hotel-café to enjoy the hotel's speciality, the most famous chocolate cake in the world. This delicious speciality reveals nothing of the bitter cake war that Sacher fought against the Demel confectioners over the name "Original Sachertorte" – and successfully: Sacher won and business is flourishing. Kärntner Strasse is generally an expensive shopping street, with one store next to another. These include the J & L Lobmeyr glass store (No. 26), which also contains a glass museum and bears the inscription "Former supplier to the Royal and Imperial Court", just like the home textiles supplier Backhausen (No. 33). The many Mozart Kugeln chocolate and marzipan balls and Mozart Becher delicacies in the "Steffl"

department store are not just a chance reminder of the composer, for it was in the house that used to stand on this spot that he died in 1791.
Like Graben and Kohlmarkt, Kärntner Strasse is a pedestrian zone, crowded with tourists, shoppers and strollers, with onlookers surrounding the many street artists and buskers. There are hardly any historic buildings in this street. The only one worth mentioning is the *Palais Esterházy* dating back to the 17th century and now home to the "Cercle" *Casino* and the Adlmüller exclusive fashion house (No. 41). Instead, the side alleys are worth a look. Himmelpfortgasse, for instance, where at No. 3 stands the sumptuous *Winter Palace of Prince Eugen*, where the great military leader died in 1736. Today, the building is the headquarters of the Ministry of Finance,

Previous double page: View from Parliament of the Town Hall and the Votive Church.

Above: View from the Town hall of the National Theatre and City Centre.

and only the famous splendid staircase is accessible to the public. A little further down the pedestrian zone, to the left, is the partly hidden Kärntner Durchgang with the *American Bar*, designed by Adolf Loos in 1907 and surviving practically unchanged. Kärntner Strasse ends at Stephansplatz, the heart of Vienna. Immediately to the left, in an alcove of the house on the corner (Palais Equitable, with a very interesting courtyard worth visiting), is the tree stump that gave its name to the square, "Stock im Eisen" (Stick in the iron). Around 1440, a fir tree was felled here, and the locksmiths declared it the symbol of their guild. Every journeyman setting off on the road hit a nail into the stump before leaving. In more recent years, the workers on the underground railway are alleged to have immortalised themselves here. Opposite stands the hotly disputed *Haas-Haus*, designed in 1985–90 by the top Viennese architect Hans Hollein. "Are they allowed to do that?" asked many a horrified Viennese at the sight of their "Steffl" (the nickname for the cathedral) faced by this post-modern construction of shining chrome and glass. Indeed they were. And of course there is no accounting for taste. In any event, nowadays the curious crowds throng eagerly into the elegant shopping centre, whose upper storey houses an excellent restaurant, a bar and a café and terrace with a magnificent view.

In the Dorotheum: Pawnshop, auction house, art gallery and bank in one.

The Haas Haus marks the beginning of *Graben*, another boulevard in the heart of Vienna. Its existence is actually thanks to the English, for the razing of the old city moat was financed using part of the huge ransom that the Austrians had received for releasing the kidnapped Richard the Lionheart. Half street, half square, Graben, together with Kohlmarkt, forms the most elegant shopping and strolling area of Vienna. It is here that the most sophisticated and most expensive stores are to be found – including a whole gaggle of former suppliers to the Royal and Imperial Court: the jeweller Heldwein (founded 1902), the Konditorei Lehmann, the Denk porcelain house (founded 1702), the G. B. Filz Sohn perfumery (founded 1809) or the Kniže fashion store (built by Loos from 1910–13). It is here that the world meets in the spreading street cafés, or strolls under palms that give the street its pleasant turn-of-the-century flair. For a long time, Graben was also home to the oldest profession in the world with its much-sung "Graben nymphs". The *Café de l'Europe* could tell many a tale. At the beginning of the century, the middle classes would meet here in the ever-crowded coffee-house by day, and the glittering demimonde would gather by night. From spring 1933 they were joined by the political emigrants from Germany, who chose the café as their nightly meeting point, amongst them Bert Brecht and Walter Mehring, before most of these visitors then fled into exile. The *l'Europe* is still worth a visit, firstly because the coffee is still roasted in the house, and secondly because of the magnificent view of Graben from the first storey. In the middle of the square stands the Baroque *Plague Column* (also known as the Trinity Column), the consequence of a solemn oath made by Emperor Leopold I when the plague claimed roughly 100,000 victims in Vienna in 1679. The centre of the square contains another interesting sight, the wonderfully restored Jugendstil WC designed by Adolf Loos (not the origin of the English word for this establishment), worth paying a visit even if you don't "have to".When on Graben, the many side alleys make an interesting detour. Dorotheergasse alone contains several places of interest: the popular Trzesniewski snack bar, then the *Café Hawelka*, the legendary artists' café of the 1960s, whose sparkle, although faded, still

remains today, the Jewish Museum and finally the *Dorotheum*, the "pawn shop", a Viennese institution from the time when pawning one's treasures was the only way to survive. Founded in the former Convent of the Sisters of St. Dorothy in 1707 by Emperor Joseph I as "Versatz- und Fragamt zu Wien" (Pawning and Pledging Office in Vienna), today the Dorotheum is the sixth largest auction house in the world, a remarkable cross between pawn shop, art gallery, auction house and bank. Major art auctions take place here four times a year. However, one can submerge oneself every day in the creaky atmosphere of this building and observe the fortune-seekers at the regular auctions of all kinds of goods. Everything is here, from valuable Jugendstil to charming junk. Many a bargain can also be made in over-the-counter trade.
A little further towards Kohlmarkt, Jungferngasse leads off to the right from Graben to the *Peterskirche* (St. Peter's Church). The Baroque building with its mighty dome was designed by Johann Lukas von Hildebrandt in 1703–08, and harmonises perfectly with the narrow streets of the old city. At the end of November, beginning of December the church houses a display of Christmas cribs with a very special atmosphere of its own.
At the end of Graben and to the right is "Tuchlauben", with the Gothic *Neidhart Frescos* at No. 19, a sight well worth the detour. Around 1400, a rich cloth merchant had his hall painted with images from the poems of the Minnesänger (troubadour) Neidhart von Reuenthal. Subsequently covered over and partially destroyed, these oldest secular paintings of Vienna were discovered accidentally in 1979. To the left at the end of Graben is the fashionable *Kohlmarkt*, which betrays no trace whatsoever of its grimy beginnings as Vienna's charcoal market. It is now the home of everything that is good and expensive. The Retti candle store at and the Schullin jeweller's were designed by the architect Hans Hollein. They stand side by side with the Jugendstil building of the Artaria publishing company, where Chopin stayed during his visits to Vienna. No. 14 houses the famous *Demel* Royal and Imperial Court Confectioner's, the most noble representative of this institution in Vienna. Here you are not served by simple waitresses but by "Demelinerinnen" in their traditional black dresses with white collars, who still address their customers with a humble "Haben schon gewählt?" (Has Sir/Madam chosen?). The establishment is almost a temple for the sweet-toothed. The windows display the unbelievable works of art of the confectioners in opulently designed displays based on the season or on current events. Founded in 1857 and transferred to Kohlmarkt 30 years later, the house can look back on a very turbulent past, the most unpleasant chapter without doubt involving the one-time owner Udo Proksch. This adventurer and social lion was the origin of one of the greatest political scandals of the Second Republic at the beginning of the 1990s. The sinking of the freighter "Lucona", which he arranged and which claimed six lives in an insurance fraud, cost not only its perpetrator his freedom but also the positions of a number of leading politicians with whom he was friends – a group that previously met as the "Club 44" in a backroom of the elegant Demel.

Viennese night-life: in the Loos Bar.

Imperial Vienna

From Graben, Kohlmarkt leads to Michaelerplatz, a square that brings together a number of different eras. The middle of the square contains remains from 1,000 years of Viennese building history, from the Roman era through the Middle Ages and up to the 19th century. To the left is the old *Michaeler Kirche* (St. Michael's Church), the former court parish church of the Imperial family, whose classical facade conceals Vienna's only late Romanesque-early Gothic religious building. To the right is the *Loos-Haus* by Adolf Loos dating from 1910 and of a simplicity that originally caused a scandal, while No. 2 is the *Café Griensteidl*, the successor to the legendary literary café where Schnitzler, Baar, Hofmannsthal and many others gathered at the end of the 19th century. At the far end of the square is the splendid *Michaeler Tor* (St. Michael's Gate) with its attractive wrought ironwork. This Gate is the entrance to the *Hofburg* (Imperial Palace) – a city within the city that became the symbol of absolute power. "Not even for the palace" was the Viennese way of saying "no way". This huge monumental construction is a stylistic potpourri: the oldest part, the Schweizertrakt (Swiss Wing) is Gothic, the Stallburg Renaissance, while most of the other parts are Baroque or later imitations of other styles. Work was first begun on the building in 1275 under the rule of the Bohemian King Ottokar, who hoped thus to be prepared for the dispute with Emperor Rudolf. But the latter ultimately proved to be the stronger, and hence the Habsburgs have been documented as being "in castro Wiennensis" since 1279. Since 1533, when Ferdinand I moved his residence and all the important court offices to Vienna, all the Habsburgs have resided in the state rooms of the Hofburg.

In the crypt of St. Michael's church, where mummified corpses have survived from the 19th century.

Arriving from Michaelerplatz, the visitor first passes through the *Michaelertrakt* (St. Michael's Wing), constructed after the demolition of the old Hofburg theatre in 1888, and based on plans by Joseph Emanuel Fischer von Erlach. Then comes the "In der Burg" courtyard with a monument to Emperor Franz II in the middle. In summer, the Café Silberkammer sets up its chairs and tables here. To the right is the

View from the roof of the Museum of Fine Arts of St. Michael's dome in the Imperial Palace.

Baroque *Reichskanzleitrakt* (Imperial Chancery Wing) with the Franz Joseph apartments, open to the public as are the rooms of Tsar Alexander I and Empress Elisabeth in the adjoining Renaissance *Amalienburg* (Amalia Wing). This is followed by the *Leopoldinische Trakt* (Leopold Wing) constructed in 1660–80 and containing the residential and ceremonial apartments of Empress Maria Theresia and her son Joseph II, which cannot be visited since it now contains the official rooms of the Federal President. The *Schweizertrakt* (Swiss wing), the core of the Alte Hofburg (Old Imperial Palace) derives its name from the Swiss mercenaries, and was rebuilt as a Renaissance palace by Ferdinand I. It was then that the mighty *Schweizertor* (Swiss Gate) was also constructed. The courtyard leads to the *Burgkapelle* (Royal Chapel), first mentioned in documents in 1296 and frequently rebuilt. It was once the seat of the Imperial Orchestra and the place where the Imperial Boys' Choir, the predecessor of the modern Vienna Boys' Choir, was founded in 1498 ; they still sing mass on Sundays and church holidays. The Schweizertrakt also contains the entrance to the two *Schatzkammern* (Treasuries) with their secular and ecclesiastical treasures. A passage leads from the Alte Hofburg to Heldenplatz, one of Vienna's largest squares, and one that has played an inglorious role in recent history. It was here, from the balcony of the Neue Burg, that on March 15, 1938, Adolf Hitler announced Austria's Anschluss with the German Reich to a huge and jubilant crowd of people gathered on Heldenplatz, while at the same time the first transports of political opponents were already on their way to Dachau. The square contains the equestrian statues of two Austrian military leaders, Prince Eugen (to the left, when looking from the Schweizertrakt) and Archduke Karl. The *Festsaaltrakt* (Ceremonial Hall Wing), today houses the congress centre. Next to it is the *Neue Hofburg* (New Imperial Palace), begun in the Renaissance style by the architects of the Ringstrasse, Hasenauer and Semper, in 1881, and only completed in 1926, eight years after the last Emperor had abdicated. Today it contains the reading rooms and catalogue rooms of the Austrian National Library, one of the most important libraries in the world. From the main entrance there is a magnificent panorama view from the two large museums to the left past the Parliament building as far as the Town Hall. Next to the National Library is the *Museum für Völkerkunde* (Ethnological Museum), and next to this the *Burgtor* (Palace Gates).

The performances by the world-famous Spanish Riding School take place in the Baroque Hall of the Winter Riding School.

Another complex of the Hofburg is the *Stallburg* (Stables), Vienna's most important Renaissance palace. Since Karl VI (1685–1740), this has been home to the famous Lipizzaner Horses of the Spanish (court) Riding School. The Spanish Riding Stables were founded in Vienna as early as 1572, as the precursor of the Spanish Imperial Riding School, initially using horses from southern Spain and, from 1580, the white stallions from the Imperial Stud Farm in Lipizza near Trieste. The performances by this, the oldest riding school in the world, take place in J. E. Fischer von Erlach's Baroque "White Hall" in the *Winterreitschule* (Winter Riding School).

In 1992, a huge fire destroyed the great historic *Redoutensaal*, which dates back to the 18th century, and has been the venue for many music events and festivals as well as for the CSCE conference. Only the outer facade survived, but the hall was re-opened in 1998 with a total of 22 wall paintings and a ceiling fresco by the Austrian painter Josef Mikl covering more than 400 m^2. This contemporary artist sees the paintings as "a bow to the great figures of Austrian literature" and chose texts by Ferdinand

Raimund, Johann Nestroy, Karl Kraus and Elias Canetti as the points of reference for his paintings. Not even the Riding School and the *Nationalbibliothek* (National Library) were spared by the fire, but the damage to the frescos caused during the fire-fighting has largely been remedied. Like the Redoutensaal, the Library is reached from the Josefsplatz and was originally a free-standing high Baroque building constructed according to plans by Fischer von Erlach, father and son. The magnificent ceiling fresco in the *Prunksaal* is by Daniel Gran.

State Room of the Austrian National Library.

Also reached from Josefsplatz is the *Augustinerkirche* (Augustinian Church) connected to the Hofburg. It was built in 1330–39 as a three-nave hall church and converted to the Baroque at a later date, with the interior being re-gothicised in the 18th century. Of particular interest is the beautiful classicist marble tomb made by Antonio Canova in 1798–1805 for Archduchess Marie-Christine, a daughter of Maria Theresia and wife of Archduke Albert von Sachsen-Teschen, the founder of the Albertina Collection of Graphic Arts close by. From 1634 to 1783 the church was the imperial parish church of the Habsburgs, the scene of splendid imperial weddings and still today of ceremonial high masses and sung masses.

The Loretto chapel contains the *Herzgrüftl* (Vault of Hearts), in which the hearts of the Habsburg sovereigns are kept in 54 silver urns. The largest urn contains the hearts of Maria Theresia and her husband Franz Stephan von Lothringen. A smaller urn contains the heart of the Duke of Reichstadt, the son of Napoleon, who died in Vienna. It remained here when Adolf Hitler had the Duke's body transferred to Paris, probably because the Germans were unaware of the heart's existence and no Viennese bothered to mention it to them.

Diagonally across Lobkowitzplatz is the *Palais Lobkowitz*, a monumental Baroque construction that was a major cultural centre of 19th century Vienna. It was here that Beethoven's Eroica Symphony was first performed in 1803, and his *4th Symphony* in 1807. Since 1991, the Palais has been home to the *Österreichische Theatermuseum* (Austrian Museum of Theatre).

The Albertina *Collection of Graphic Art* is to be found on Albertinaplatz. The square itself is dominated by the *Memorial against War and Fascism* created by Alfred Hrdlicka from 1988–91. It was erected here as a memorial to the victims of the National Socialist regime and to the victims of the bombardments of the Second World War, buried under the square in filled-in underground air-raid shelters. The stone *Tor der Gewalt* (Gate of Violence) symbolises Nazi terror and the marble Orpheus represents the downfall in the War. The bronze statue of the kneeling Jew is a reminder of how the Viennese, in close collaboration with the Germans, humiliated the Jews and

compelled them to clean the streets with toothbrushes – a memorial that is disputed, and not only in the Jewish community.
Not far away is the *Kapuzinerkirche* (Church of the Capuchin Friars), with, in its vault, the tombs of the Habsburg family. Commenced in 1622 and subsequently expanded, the Kaisergruft (Imperial Burial Vault) contains 12 Emperors, 16 Empresses and over 100 Archdukes in 138 metal coffins. The last burial took place in 1989, when Ex-Empress Zita was interred under the lights of the press and television. According to the custom of "burying an Emperor at various places" practised until 1878, the bodies of the Habsburgs are here, while their inner organs are kept in urns in the Princes' or Dukes' vault in the Stephansdom. As already mentioned, their hearts are kept in the Augustinerkirche – a Baroque memento mori in a city that indeed has a special relationship with death.
The dark vaults contrast with the lively and noisy *Neue Markt* (New Market), the second-oldest market place in the city after the Hohe Markt, and with the Baroque *Donner Brunnen* (Donner Fountain) – real name the *Providentia Fountain* – in the middle; this was the first entirely secular fountain in the city, constructed by the sculptor Georg Raphael Donner in 1739.

Through Medieval Vienna

Stephansplatz has always been the heart of the city: traffic junction, gathering place, meeting point and resting place in the heart of the hectic, noise and bustle; on New Years Eve it attracts thousands who wait for the "Pummerin", the bell of the *Stephansdom* (St. Steven's Cathedral) to ring in the New Year. The cathedral itself is *the* symbol of Vienna, and its number one tourist attraction. The architect Adolf Loos wrote of it: "We have the most solemn church in the world. It is not a dead piece of the inventory that we have taken over from our fathers. This building tells us our history. Every generation has worked on it, each in their own language."
Today's main entrance to the cathedral, the Riesentor (Giant's Gate), was once only opened on special occasions and only for the high nobility. Like the two *Heidentürme* (Towers of the Heathens) on either side, it is part of the old late Romanesque church that was first mentioned in 1295. To the right of the door the abbreviation O5 can still be seen scratched into the masonry, the symbol of a resistance group against Hitler towards the end of the Second World War (5 represents E, the fifth letter of the alphabet, i. e. OE = Ö for Österreich – Austria).
The vestibule of the cathedral presents a view of the three-nave interior, with, to the left, the *Tirna Chapel* containing the tomb of Prince Eugen. The central nave contains the magnificent pulpit, a masterpiece of late Gothic sculpture by Anton Pilgram, himself immortalised here as the "Peeping Tom". Pilgram created another self-portrait on the organ pedestal he made (left nave), where he is seen holding a compass and a set-square. This is where the *Nordturm* (North Tower), also known as the *Adlerturm* (Eagle's Tower) stands. It was begun in 1450, and as legend tells, its builder Hans Puchsbaum made a pact with the devil to ensure its rapid completion; unable to keep the pact, he fell to his death from the scaffolding and the tower remained unfinished. It was finally topped off with a cupola crowned by an eagle. A lift takes visitors up to see the new "Pummerin", which has been rung since 1957 on special occasions such as the ringing in of the New

The coffins in the Imperial Burial Vault of the Capuchin Church require continuous restoration.

Year. The old bell weighed over 20 tons and was cast in 1711 from the metal of captured Turkish cannons. In 1945, however, it crashed to the ground and was smashed during the cathedral fire.
A little further on we reach the northern Tower Hall, with the "Zahnweh-Herrgott" (God of Toothache) on the wall. This figure in pain is said to have punished three petty criminals with toothache, and since then is said to provide protection against this infliction. Here too is the stairway down to the *Katakomben* (Catacombs). After the plague of 1713, when all the cemeteries were more than full, around 11,000 corpses were thrown into the shafts and walled in as soon as the vaults were full. It was only later that convicts and monks sorted through the bones. The centre point is the Duke's Vault, which Rudolf IV had constructed for the Habsburgs. However, after the Kapuzinergruft was built, only the urns containing the internal organs were kept here. The catacombs (closed under Joseph II) were opened to the public in the 19th century, attracting huge throngs, particularly during the year of the World Exhibition (1873).
Alongside the empty founder's tomb constructed for Rudolf IV, the left chancel contains the Wiener Neustadt Altarpiece (1447). The main altar (1640–60) was made of black marble by the brothers Tobias and Johann Jakob Pock. The Gothic glass windows to the right and left behind the altar have survived through the centuries. The south chancel is dominated by the sumptuous marble tomb of Emperor Friedrich III, with its mysterious motto "AEIOU". In front of the main altar, to the right by a pillar stands the magnificent "Servant's Madonna" (1325) on a small pedestal (in front of the organ). This early Gothic sculpture was donated when a serving maid

The Pummerin, weighing over 20 tonnes, is rung only to welcome in the New Year and on special occasions.

View of the main altar in St. Stephen's Cathedral.

accused of theft asked the Virgin for help, whereupon the true perpetrator was allegedly discovered; since then the Madonna has been prayed to in the event of injustice. On the way back to the Riesentor, near to the exit, there is an altar containing the "miracle-working image of the Virgin of Pötsch", an icon from the Hungarian village of Pócs near Eger dating back to 1697. Ever since the battle of Zenta in 1697, the image has been highly revered in both Austria and Hungary. Prince Eugen was victorious in this decisive battle in the Turkish War, and throughout the two weeks that it lasted, tears are said to have flowed from the Virgin's eyes.
The stairs up the *Südturm* (South Tower) are outside the cathedral. 136.7 m tall, the "Steffl" is the third highest church tower in the world and is regarded as one of the most beautiful of the German Gothic period. Completed in 1433, it was long the guardian of the city, containing a fire brigade look-out from 1534 to 1956, while today, after a climb of the 343 steps to the Türmerstube, there is a magnificent panorama of the roof tops and roof-gardens of the city. In 1973, the mysterious Virgil Chapel was discovered during building work for the underground railway, and is now to be seen from the Stephansplatz underground station – a view into the middle ages 12 metres under the ground. The underground chapel with the largest surviving Gothic interior in Vienna was constructed in 1250 beneath the old Mary Magdalen Chapel, the outline of which is to be seen in the cobblestones of Stephansplatz. The room – claimed by esoterics to be a "place of positive energy" – is today a small museum that also includes a small collection presenting nine centuries of Viennese ceramics.
The Weihburggasse leads to the romantic *Franziskanerplatz* with its self-contained ensemble of buildings dating from the 17th and 18th centuries. In the summer a fountain splashes away in the middle, and the tables and chairs of the "Kleine Café", one of the first fashionable establishments of Vienna, are set out here in the open air.
The square is dominated by the Franziskanerkirche (Church of the Franciscan Friars),

Vienna's only religious building with a Renaissance facade. It also houses the oldest organ in the city (1643). The main altar shows a painting of *Madonna with the Axe*: allegedly, a Protestant iconoclast attempted to destroy the picture but the axe caught fast in the painting and the perpetrator died.

Not far from Franziskanerplatz is Grünangergasse, where, on the house on the corner to Singerstrasse, there is a plaque in memory of the dramatist Franz Grillparzer, who lived and worked here for a time. No. 8 deals with matters much more prosaic. It is alleged that it was in the "Kipfelhaus" in 1683 that – perhaps as a mockery of the crescent moon of the Turkish besieging army – the first Kipferl (croissant) was baked. *Blutgasse* runs parallel to this street, and is one of the most beautiful and oldest alleys; its name possibly derives from the fact that the blood of the Knights Templar flowed through this street during a massacre in 1312. The alley leads directly to the *Figaro Haus*, Vienna's only Mozart residence still in original condition.

Strobelgasse and Essiggasse then take us into Bäckerstrasse, an area with a wide selection of bars and restaurants for lovers of night-life. Of interest is the *Schwanfeldsche Haus* (No. 7) with the most beautiful Renaissance courtyard in the city, enchanting the visitor with its quiet arcades wreathed in vines. It was only in 1770 that houses in Vienna were given numbers; until then there had only been painted house symbols such as the fragments of a cow and a wolf playing backgammon at Bäckerstrasse 12; the two animals represent Protestantism and Catholicism, while between them stands a furrier (a caricature of the opportunism of the city council) waiting to see who will win. Who won is only too apparent at the Dr. Ignaz Seipel Platz, only a few steps away. The Baroque *Jesuit Church* and the *Old University*, once run by the Jesuits, bear overwhelming witness to the triumph of the Counter-reformation.

The picturesque *Schönlaterngasse* derives its name ("Alley of the beautiful lantern") from the house symbol on No. 6, a "beautiful lantern". No. 7's house symbol is a basilisk, a monster that once lived in the house well and terrified the residents way back in 1212, until one day a mirror was put in front of its face, and the monster burst in terror at its own ugliness. So goes the legend at least, the oldest in the city.

The next building is the *Alte Schmiede* (old forge), an ancient vault with a display of blacksmith's tools and the venue of the "literary quarter" with regular readings, musical events and exhibitions.

An archway leads into the spacious *Heiligenkreuzerhof*, the city residence of the old Heiligenkreuz monastery near Vienna. Baroque buildings surround the quiet, spacious square, where the noise and bustle of the city are totally unknown. On the other side of the courtyard, a gate leads out into the city and to Fleischmarkt. Here, next-door to the Greek Orthodox Church at No. 13, is the famous *Griechenbeisl* (Greek Tavern). Established in 1490 and thus probably the oldest tavern in Vienna, it was called "Zum roten Dachl" (At the sign of the red roof) at the end of the 18th century, and only acquired its modern name much later with the arrival of the many Greeks who took up residence in the area. Amongst the tavern's guests have been Mozart, Beethoven, Strauss and Schubert, Grillparzer and Nestroy as well as Graf Zeppelin. It was here that Mark Twain wrote his story "*The One Million Pound Note*". And allegedly the Liebe Augustin was a regular guest here, that old Viennese street singer who, so the legend goes, at the time of the plague in 1679 one night fell drunk into a ditch full of plague corpses to sleep off his intoxication, only to be pulled out the next day, completely unharmed, by the plague workers. Since then he has served as the symbol of the fact that you can't keep a "genuine Viennese" down. The restaurant has an atmosphere all its own, and consists of seven small rooms, one of which is the "artists' parlour", with a ceiling completely covered with countless famous signatures from across the centuries: from Prince Eugen to Bismarck, Mozart to Brahms, Johnny Cash to Johnny Weissmüller – and the waiter will patiently list them all as he points to them with his long stick, even if you are not a guest at all but just a curious passer by ...

From Vindobona to Vienna

The starting point is what is popularly known as the *Bermuda Triangle*, a maze of bars, restaurants and pubs near the Danube Canal, where allegedly, as in the genuine Bermuda Triangle, many a person has disappeared without trace for the night. From here, Seitenstättengasse and its conglomeration of bars leads uphill, past the *Synagogue* and the Jewish Community Centre, a classicist building by Josef Kornhäusl, the leading architect of the Viennese Biedermeier. The City Temple was constructed in 1826 and complied with the imperial regulation that Jewish and Protestant houses of God should not have a conspicuous street front but must be hidden in a residential building. It was this provision that saved the Temple during the 1938 November Pogrom, when all the synagogues went up in flames. Since the Nazis did not wish to endanger the residential building, this temple was the only one to survive in Vienna; however, the interior was completely devastated.

Service in the synagogue in Seitenstettengasse.

At its end, the street widens for the small Romanesque *Ruprechtskirche* (St. Rupert's Church), the oldest religious building in Vienna, first mentioned in documents in 1161. The small square in front of the church provides a view down to Morzinplatz. What is now the patch of lawn was once the site of the Hotel Metropol, the headquarters of the Gestapo during the Third Reich. Countless Viennese were tortured and murdered here during interrogations, as is witnessed today by a commemorative plaque.
Desider Friedmann Platz, not far from the Ruprechtskirche, is named after the last President of the Jewish religious community before 1938; here stands the smooth and mighty *Kornhäuselturm* (Kornhäusel Tower) that the architect Kornhäusel constructed as his home in 1827. Judengasse with its many small boutiques and the kosher restaurant Arche Noah, leads to Hohe Markt, where stands the Baroque *Vermählungsbrunnen* (Wedding Fountain) erected in 1729 by Leopold I. This oldest square in the city was once the centre of the Roman town of Vindobona, as shown by the excavations here. There is a further reminder of the Roman Emperor Marcus Aurelius on the *Ankeruhr* (Anker clock) high above between houses Nos. 10–11 and 12, where he makes his daily appearance together with 12 other persons of importance for Vienna. Each hour one of the figures is displayed, from Marcus Aurelius via the Minnesänger Walther von der Vogelweide to Joseph Haydn. Only at twelve o'clock midday do all appear together. This popular work of art was "dedicated to the Viennese" in 1914 by the Anker Insurance Company.
Hohe Markt was once a place of executions, and until as late as 1839 the de-

cisions of the court were announced from the balcony of the Schranne (Court Building). And it was probably on this square that Otto Haymo, the founder of the *Salvatorkapelle* (Chapel of the Saviour) just around the corner in Wipplingerstrasse met his death. This freedom-loving citizen was one of the leaders of a conspiracy that hoped to liberate the city from the Habsburgs after the murder of King Albrecht I (1308). The chapel has a magnificent Renaissance portal and is next-door to the *Alte Rathaus* (Old Town Hall). After the conspiracy had been exposed, Friedrich the Beautiful gave the building to the City Council, which used it as a Town Hall until the new building was constructed on Ringstrasse. Today it contains the *Dokumentationsarchiv des Österreichischen Widerstandes* (Documentary Archives of the Austrian Resistance), whose exhibits testify to the resistance against the Austro-Fascist dictatorship (1934–38) and National Socialism (1938–45). This district also contains the church of *Maria am Gestade* (Virgin on the Shore). The church, whose front is reminiscent of the bow of a ship, once stood on the steep slope of a branch of the Danube, and was originally the church of the Danube raftsmen. The steep steps down to Tiefer Graben still give an idea of the slope, and explain why it was here that both the Roman Fort and the early medieval town were located: Hohe Markt and its surroundings lay on a protected high plateau. The church building as it is today, a jewel of Gothic architecture, dates back to the 14th century. Particularly impressive are the two high-gothic panel paintings of the Annunciation and the Coronation of the Virgin, as well as the surviving fragments of medieval glass painting. These contrast with the shrine containing the relics of Saint Klemens Maria Hofbauer (1751–1820), the patron saint of Vienna.
Between the church of Maria am Gestade and the Danube Canal is the so called *"textiles quarter"*, a traditional Jewish quarter with numerous clothes and textile stores selling cheap goods both wholesale and retail around Rudolfsplatz.
Judenplatz was the centre of the Jewish district in the middle ages, and it was here that the *Or-Sarua Synagogue* stood, with one of the most important Talmud schools of the German-speaking world; the remains were uncovered and displayed in 1995/

The Romanesque St. Rupert's Church is the oldest church in Vienna.

Maria am Gestade: In the middle ages, a branch of the Danube flowed directly below the church.

1996. Some of the houses on the square have survived unchanged, e.g. No. 1, in which Franz Grillparzer wrote his drama *"Das goldene Vlies"* (The Golden Fleece) in 1818/19, while others, such as No. 3–4, where Mozart lived for a time, were combined or renovated. The Jewish quarter was destroyed during the first Viennese Gesera in 1421, when 210 Jews perished miserably, burned to death. A notorious Latin inscription in the late Gothic relief of the Baptism of Christ on the *Haus zum Grossen Jordan* (the House of the Great Jordan) (No. 2), the oldest building on the square, dating back to the 15th century, refers to this event: " ... and thus in the year 1421 the flames of hate sprang up, devastated the city and expiated the dreadful crimes of the Hebrew dogs." The *Lessing Memorial* in the centre of the square, intended as a reminder of humanism and tolerance, was removed and melted down by the Nazis in 1938. It was reconstructed and stood on the Morzinplatz from 1968, and only in 1982, and not without public commotion, was it returned to its original place. There was also considerable uproar about a memorial plaque deliberately erected here in 1998 as the first reminder of the Catholic church's partial responsibility for the persecution of the Jews in the middle ages. The new Holocaust memorial by Rachel Whitbread on this square was also preceded by vehement controversy, particularly after the remains of the synagogue were discovered. Finally, the city administration gave the go-ahead in 1998 for the construction of the memorial, but resolved to leave access open to the excavations. Not far from here lies the Schulhof. This quiet square seems bewitched, and when a fiacre clatters by occasionally, time seems to have been standing still since the last century. And indeed it is here, in the Harfenhaus, that the *Clock Museum* of the City Of Vienna is housed. For inexhaustible museum fanatics, right next-door is the *Museum of Dolls and Toys*. A few steps further on is the broad square *Am Hof* with its splendid Baroque ensemble. Here in the 12th century was the oldest Babenberg Palace, whose magnificent court (Hof – hence the name of the square) inspired the Minnesinger Walther von der Vogelweide to enthuse about the "wünneclîchen Hof ze Wiene" (the wonderful court in Vienna). The square is dominated by the individualistic early Baroque facade of the former Jesuit church *Zu den Neun Chören der Engel* (The Nine Choirs of Angels) – a historical spot, for it was from the balcony that an imperial commissioner announced the end of the Holy Roman Empire in 1806. No. 10, the former *Bürgerliche Zeughaus* (Civilian Arsenal) contains the fire-brigade headquarters and also provides access to the excavations of the *Am Hof Roman Ruins*, while the Märkleinschen Haus (No. 7) houses the *Fire-Brigade Museum*. At the exit from the square, to the right of the "Heidenschuss" (Heathen's Shot), is the *Kunstforum Bank Austria* (Bank Austria Art Forum) – a private exhibition centre that holds excellent temporary exhibitions of famous Austrian and international artists. Beyond this is *Freyung*, a triangular square whose focal point is the *Austria Fountain*, a reminder of the country's past glories in the form of allegories of the four main rivers of the monarchy, the Po, the Elbe, the Vistula and the Danube. The large building at No. 7, known for its façade as the *Schubladenkastenhaus* ("Chest of Drawers" house), dates back to 1774. The square is dominated by the *Schottenstift* (Monastery of the Scots), named after the "Scots", who in reality where Irish monks. The Babenberg Duke Heinrich II Jasomirgott (derived from his motto "Ja so mir Gott helfe" [Yes, God help me]), had invited them to Vienna, where they founded their monastery in 1155. The extensive building contains amongst other things the Schottengymnasium, one of the most famous schools in the city, a guest house and an interesting museum in which pride of place goes to the late Gothic winged altarpiece by the "Viennese Scots Master". Freyung is a popular market place today: every second weekend it hosts the largest organic farmer's market in Austria, against a background of magnificent baroque palaces such as the Palais Kinsky, a building by the master architect Johann Lukas von Hildebrandt. The neighbouring Palais Ferstel was designed by its original owner, the celebrated Ringstrasse architect Heinrich Ferstel; the glass-roofed passage between Herrengasse and Freyung is a reminder of the large European shopping arcades that were in fashion at the time. It houses a number of elegant stores and a new version of the legendary *Café Central*, which was the meeting point for literary Vienna at the turn of the century.

It is here that the Herrengasse, Bankgasse and Wallnergasse district begins, chock-a-block with the palaces of the high nobility: Modena, Batthyány, Esterházy, Trautson – anyone who was anyone had their residence here behind the impressive facades. Behind these old palaces stands Minoritenplatz, where, dominated by the characteristic tower of the *Minoritenkirche* (Church of the Friars Minor), a simple memorial recalls the great Viennese painter Rudolf von Alt. Inside the "Italian National Church of Mary of the Snows", as it has been officially called since 1786, there is a copy of Leonardo da Vinci's *Last Supper*. Napoleon had ordered it from the Roman mosaic artist Giacomo Raffaelli in 1809, when his troops occupied Vienna. Since the work was to be created using tiny mosaic stones, it was, however, only completed after the French Emperor had already been overthrown. It was finally acquired by the Viennese court. Moreover, the painting on the main altar is also a copy, with the original, *Mary of the Snows*, hanging in Rome. And there is a further link to Italy: the Roman poet Pietro Metastasio, a court poet of Maria Theresia, is buried in this church.

On the square behind the church there is a

The church of the Friars Minor – in simple contrast to the Baroque splendour of the surrounding palaces.

bust of Leopold Figl, the first Federal Chancellor after the Second World War and the father of the Austrian State Treaty that ended the occupation of Austria by the allied powers in 1955. From here Bruno Kreisky Gasse, named after the famous statesman of the second republic, leads to the politically highly significant *Ballhausplatz*. No. 2, built by the Baroque master J. L. von Hildebrandt, was initially the home of the Secret Imperial Chancellery, and later the State Chancellery. During the Congress of Vienna 1814/15 it was the scene of many an important meeting. It was here, too, that the ultimatum to Serbia was drafted in 1914, thus triggering the First World War. And it was here in 1934 that Federal Chancellor Engelbert Dollfuss, whose government seat this was, was murdered during an attempted putsch by the National Socialists. Today this representational building houses the Federal Chancellor's Office and the Foreign Ministry.

Between the Ring and the Gürtel

From the Hundertwasser Haus to Schloss Belvedere

In 1983–85, Friedensreich Hundertwasser, one of Austria's most prominent painters, was finally allowed to carry out a public housing project for the city council using ideas he had long been pushing: irregularity instead of "godless" straight lines, the natural cycle of digestion and growth in the compost toilet, the "afforestation of the cities". Accordingly, the architect Josef Krawina prepared a "green" concept for the building, which included an energy-saving construction method, organically healthy materials and additional facilities such as indoor swimming-pool, sauna and organic food store. It was intended to be a "house that meets the needs of nature and man", and in any event is a spectacular building. The apartments seem to be stacked on top of each other like colourful little towers. The floors are uneven, the walls crooked, the edges rounded. The "weapon of the architect's ruler" seems indeed to have been left unused. Trees and flowers flourish on the little balconies, terraces, flat roofs, and even from many a window. Hundertwasser wanted to build a living house. He succeeded, and every day visitors from all over the world flood in to marvel at this cheerful organic castle. What cannot be seen, of course, is how the people live in the over 50 apartments that this council building contains. Only the terrace cafe is open to the public. Instead, opposite in Kegelgasse, is Hundertwasser's *Kalke Village*, once a horse mail depot, today a souvenir hunter's paradise with café, gallery and exchange office, all surrounded by plenty of greenery. Just around the corner, Hundertwasser – ever the smart businessman – has expanded his "fantastic" realm with the *KunstHausWien* (Art House Vienna). Here, occupying an area of 3,500 m^2 in the former premises of the traditional furniture company Thonet, an exhibition of works by Hundertwasser can be seen alongside international temporary exhibitions (including very interesting photography exhibitions!). On the ground floor there is another Hundertwasser shop and a cosy restaurant with an attractive garden.

This house was designed by the great philosopher Ludwig Wittgenstein for his sister Margarethe Stonborough.

The Hundertwasser House, built 1983–85, the realisation of the painter's idea of building "close to nature".

From here the route leads away from the city centre as far as the Café Zartl, a well-known Viennese coffee-house, and then to the quiet of the elegant "embassy district" (the British, German, Italian, Russian and Chinese embassies among others are fairly close by). There is an example of a completely different approach to architecture, the *Wittgenstein House* – a wide cubic building in the style of Adolf Loos, the artist Hundertwasser attacked in his 1968 criticism of architecture. The philosopher Ludwig Wittgenstein built the house from 1926 to 1929 together with his friend, the Loos pupil Paul Engelmann, for his sister Margarethe Stonborough-Wittgenstein. In its severity and simplicity it reflects the logical clarity of Wittgenstein's thinking, and for this reason it has been described as "logic turned to stone". What must Wittgenstein have thought of the fact that his sister, who was also an acquaintance of Sigmund Freud, should choose to decorate this minimalist home with a decorative portrait by Klimt? The building was subsequently forgotten. A military hospital during the war, it was to have been pulled down and replaced by a hotel after the death of its owner in 1958. Demolition was only prevented by a vigorous rescue campaign, and it was placed under historic monument protection in 1971. It was finally acquired by the Bulgarian embassy and restored, and now serves as a cultural institute; the entrance in Parkgasse also offers the best view of the building. Less well-known is the unusual *Karl Borromäus Brunnen* (Charles Borromeus Fountain) stands. It was erected by the sculptor Josef Engelhart, one of the founders of the Secession, and the Slovene architect Josip Plecnik in 1904. A simple obelisk stands in the heart of this small, idyllic square, surrounded by the attractive clover-leaf fountain; three groups of figures tell the story of St. Charles Borromeus, the patron saint of the Karlskirche. The fountain is in a hollowed circle, surrounded by benches, and is a peaceful spot for a rest in summer. The *Portois & Fix Building* in the Ungargasse is a jewel of the Jugendstil in this quarter. Designed by Max Fabiani in 1900, this house with its tiled facade is a reminder of Otto Wagner's famous Majolica House in Wienzeile.

"East of Rennweg begins the orient" as even Chancellor Metternich realised. But Rennweg is long, and leads towards Hungary. And it is hardly likely that he meant that the orient began at house No. 27, since Metternich himself lived there before he fled to England in 1848 as a victim of the revolution (today the house is the seat of the Italian embassy). Rennweg was also home to another famous house owner: in 1891, when this now traffic-plagued street was still a top address, the architect Otto Wagner built himself a city house at No. 3. It is now known as the Palais Hoyos and houses the embassy of the Federal Republic of Yugoslavia. The two neighbouring houses are also by Wagner; one of them (No. 5) was the home of the composer Gustav Mahler from 1898 to 1909. Next to it is the *Gardekirche* (Church of the Guard), constructed in 1763 by Maria Theresia's court architect Nicolaus Pacassi, who also redesigned Schönbrunn. The church, converted six years later in the Classicist style, still contains the original, partially gilded Rococo stucco decoration. In 1782, the church was given to the Polish Guard, and is today Vienna's Polish national church. Every Sunday, 8 masses are said in Polish in the crowded church, and another two in the *Salesianerinnen Kirche* (Church of the Salesian Nuns), only a few steps further down the road and directly next to the exit from the Lower Belvedere. This church, constructed with the assistance of Joseph Emanuel Fischer von Erlach, is an attractive Baroque building crowned by an impressive dome.

The Upper Belvedere, former summer palace of Prince Eugen.

Leaving Rennweg, the visitor first comes to the *Untere Belvedere* (Lower Belvedere) (Rennweg 6), externally a much more modest construction compared with the Belvedere on the hill that gave it its name. The buildings and park were all built for Prince Eugen of Savoy, who was of French origin and one of Austria's most successful military leaders. Apparently, the Habsburgs were willing to pay quite a price for his victories against the French and the Turks, for at any rate the highly educated statesman – with Versailles in mind – was able to afford this representational summer residence in the form of two Baroque palaces facing each other (the lower palace as a residence, the upper as a palace of delights), which, together with the parks, exotic menagerie and birdhouse, he commissioned from Johann Lukas von Hildebrandt.

Built in 1716, the lower building's splendid

The Austrian gallery in the Upper Belvedere: in the foreground Max Klinger's "Kauernde", in the background Gustav Klimt's "The Violet Hat".

interior is a surprise. As in the Upper Belvedere, its centre is formed by a richly decorated marble room. Also of interest are the Gold Cabinet (Hall of mirrors with gilded panelling) and the Marble Gallery. The *Baroque Museum* in the building contains numerous treasures including works by leading 17th and 18th century Austrian painters, the original lead figures for Georg R. Donner's fountain on the Neue Markt and the grotesque character-study heads by Franz Xaver Messer-schmidt. The attached Orangerie, which served as stables under Maria Theresia, today contains the *Museum of Medieval Austrian Art* with its Romanesque and Gothic carvings and altar pieces.
The magnificent *Gardens* climb in a number of stages from the Lower to the Upper Belvedere, and are dominated by majestic fountains and waterworks. Still largely in their original form, the gardens are one of the greatest examples of Baroque garden art, their artfulness only revealed to the full if one climbs from the Lower to the *Upper Belvedere*: as one follows the central alley in front of the residential palace, it appears to hover over the cascades of water, drawing the visitor forward as if by magic. The way up is along two side alleys, littered with numerous stone statues, providing an oblique view of the palace as it comes nearer and nearer, and of the masterly arrangement of its constituent elements and the richly decorated facade. Having arrived at the top, there is a view of the whole of the inner city – a magnificent panorama that the painter Canaletto recorded in a famous painting now in the Kunsthistorische Museum.
The *Obere Belvedere* (Upper Belvedere) was inaugurated in 1724, and its representative exterior and sumptuous furnishing made it a grandiose setting for festivities and ceremonies. Santino Bussi's white sculpture in the Sala Terrena, Carlo Carlone's

Sphinx in the Belvedere Palace Park.

frescos in the Garden Hall and the Marble Hall alone make the climb worthwhile. The splendid Baroque building also houses the masterpieces of the *Austrian Gallery Of The 19th And 20th Centuries*. The works shown include paintings by Klimt, Schiele, Kokoschka, Waldmüller, Romako and Makart, as well as numerous Impressionists. Even during the monarchy, the Upper Belvedere was for a hundred years home to the Habsburg collection of paintings before it was moved to the newly constructed Kunsthistorisches Museum at the turn of the century. In 1894, the heir to the throne, Franz Ferdinand, moved in and lived in the Upper Belvedere until he was murdered in Sarajevo in 1914. It was in an apartment of this building that Anton Bruckner died in 1896. From 1934 to 1938, the Chancellor Kurt Schuschnigg also lived here, while after the Second World War the palace's Marble Hall witnessed the Foreign Ministers of the four occupying powers sign the State Treaty on May 15, 1955, confirming Austria's return to independence.

To the east of the palace, a stone's throw away, is the *Botanical Garden*, where Maria Theresia's personal doctor Gerard van Swieten grew medicinal herbs; today there are countless unusual plants to be seen. The adjoining *Alpine Garden* (founded in 1754) with its thousands of alpine

plants, some of them extremely rare, is worth a detour.

From the Belvedere to the Secession

Leaving the Upper Belvedere by the Prince Eugenstrasse exit, fans of the morbid side of Vienna can visit the *Bestattungsmuseum* (Funeral Museum) in the nearby Goldeggasse, with its collection of curiosities from the history of the Viennese burial tradition. And for those who are seized by longings of mortality, another detour is well worth trying, for just across Landstrasser Gürtel not far from the Südbahnhof is the *Heeresgeschichtliche Museum* (Museum of Military History) in the Arsenal. The young Emperor Franz Joseph had the *Arsenal* constructed immediately after his coronation to ensure the defence of the city so as to nip in the bud any unrest similar to that of 1848. The huge complex with its 72 buildings was constructed from 1849 to 1856 in the Historicist style by the leading lights amongst the subsequent Ringstrasse architects, and today is home to, amongst other things, the workshops of the National Theatre and the Federal Office for Public Monuments, as well as to the Heeresgeschichtliche Museum, the first museum to be opened to the public in Vienna. It was designed by Ludwig Förster and Theophil Hansen, and is seen as one of the best historical museums in Europe. Four sections show 500 years of the military history of Europe and particularly of Austria. The documentation covers the Austrian Polar Expedition from 1872 to 1874, as well as the Austro-Hungarian fleet, at the time the sixth largest in the world – an unbelievable notion in today's Alpine republic. From the Turkish siege of Vienna to the assassination in Sarajevo, this display covers all the bloody events that have had their long-term influence on the history of Europe. Amongst the most sensational exhibits is the car in which Crown Prince Franz Ferdinand and his wife Sophie were shot in Sarajevo in 1914, the couch on which he was then laid and the bloody tunic of his uniform that was cut open in order to try to save him – in vain, as we now know. In and around the building is the world's largest collection of historic gun barrels. The Schwarzenbergplatz, one of the most monumental squares of the entire Ringstrasse era, is further testimony to the horrors of war. The square is towered over by the Befreiungsdenkmahl (Liberation Memorial), a reminder of the decisive role played by the Red Army in the liberation of Vienna in April 1945. The monument, dedicated to the fallen Soviet solders, was unveiled as early as August 1945, the first

The dome of St. Charles' Church, one of the most important Baroque buildings in the city.

new construction after the liberation, and the city of Vienna undertook to maintain it. After the withdrawal of the Allied troops in 1955, the square returned to its original name, having been named the Josef Stalin Platz since 1946. Behind the monument is the *Hochstrahlbrunnen* (High-Jet Fountain) with its bizarre rock formations – illuminated in colour on summer nights. It was started up in 1873 on the occasion of the completion of the first Vienna high alpine spring water pipeline. Behind it towers Somewhat hidden on the square is the *Palais Schwarzenberg*, one of the first aristocratic summer residences constructed outside Vienna's city walls. Today among the finest and most elegant hotels in the city, this long elegant building is one of the most interesting high-Baroque aristocratic palaces in Vienna, The planning began in 1716, and involved the greatest architects of the time. The hotel contains a rich collection of works of art, with a particular jewel in the sumptuous marble hall being the ceiling frescos by Daniel Gran. There is even a genuine Rubens to be seen (Rubens Room). The building was severely damaged during the Second World War, but was skilfully restored, and has served since as a hotel. It has managed successfully to combine its princely-baroque flair with the work of renowned European architects and artists. One wing of the building is occupied by the Prince Schwarzenberg family, once one of the most powerful aristocratic families in the Monarchy and still the owners of the palace. General Carl Schwarzenberg, victor in the battle of Leipzig 1813, was immortalised by Ernst Julius Hähnel in 1867 in the equestrian statue that dominates the part of Schwarzenbergplatz by the Ring.

A very different tone is set by the *French Embassy*. This palace was built in 1906/09 according to plans by George Paul Chédanne, at the time the chef architect of the French Foreign Office; it is regarded as the main work of French *art nouveau* (equivalent to the Jugendstil) outside France.

Not far from the embassy, the Lothringerstrasse branches off, the street where Karl Kraus lived in the huge house at No. 4–8 from 1912 until his death in 1934. The street leads to *Karlsplatz*, today a huge traffic junction, intersected by roads and pedestrian subways extending from the Secession to the Opera House, and it is difficult to imagine the former charm of this square. Nevertheless, three architectural jewels defy all the attempts at modernisation: the mighty Karlskirche (Saint Charles' Church) and two delightfully restored delights from the Jugendstil era, namely the old urban railway station building by Otto Wagner and, on the other side of the square, the Secession with its shining golden leaf-patterned dome. The *Historisches Museum der Stadt Wien* (Historical Museum of the City of Vienna) is also on Karlsplatz, a building that is more functional than aesthetic, dating from the late 1950s and containing collections that provide a clear overview of Vienna's history from prehistoric times until the 20th century. Next to it towers the mighty Karlskirche, Vienna's most important religious Baroque building, and one of the landmarks of the city. Promised by Emperor Karl VI to his name saint, the patron saint of the plague, Charles Borromäus, in 1713, the year of the plague, the church was consecrated in 1737. The unique dome construction is a masterpiece by Fischer von Erlach father and son. It is almost 80 m long and 60 m wide, while the highest point of the dome is 72 m high. Remarkably, the enormous costs were

borne by all the crown lands of the monarchy. The Karlskirche was the last major architectural glorification of religious and political power, of the Habsburg Emperors and the triumphant Catholic Church. Originally constructed in a dominant position high above the steep slopes of the valley of the river Wien, the front of the church faces towards the Hofburg, the Emperor's residence. The two triumphant columns relating the life of St. Charles are over 33 m high and are topped with the unmistakable symbols of worldly power: each one bears a crown surrounded by four golden imperial eagles. In the pool in front of the church stands the sculpture *Hill Arches* by Henry Moore, a gift by the artist to the city of Vienna. The neighbouring park contains monuments to the composer Johannes Brahms (who died at nearby Karlsgasse 4) and the Austrian inventors Johann Ressel (ship's propeller), Josef Madersberger (sewing machine) and Siegfried Marcus (petrol engine).
The old *Technical University* also stands on the south side of Karlsplatz, a Classicist building constructed in 1816–18, the upper floors being added later; a new building (Wiedner Hauptstrasse 10) houses the university's main library, a huge stone owl on the outside wall acting as a post modernist figurehead.
In the middle of Karlsplatz stand the old *City Railway Station Buildings* by Otto Wagner, re-erected after the square was redesigned. One of the pavilions constructed by Wagner in 1901 and incorporating marble and gold trim is today used as an exit for the underground railway, the other as a café. The view to the Secession is blocked by a huge yellow box, intended as a merely temporary construction, the 920 m² large *Kunsthalle Wien* (Vienna Art Hall) built by Adolf Krischanitz in 1992 for exhibitions of contemporary art.
The *Naschmarkt*, Vienna's oldest and best supplied food market, extends from Karlsplatz along the Wien Valley, with some of its stalls still in the Jugendstil and inspired by oriental stands. The closer one is to the city, the more exclusive and expensive are the stalls, but the market becomes increasingly popular as one progresses. In the noise and bustle, this belly of Vienna presents a colourful image of the population of the city. The many small restaurants serving food from around the world are very popular, with fish restaurants, sushi bars, Indian, Arabic, Turkish or Italian dishes and plenty more. The Naschmarkt is an experience of its own, and it's well worth spending some time here. The crowds are worst on Saturdays, but this is also when the hustle and bustle is at its most exciting, and it is also possible to visit the peasant market and the *flea market* that are attached to the Naschmarkt on this day.
At Linke Wienzeile 6 is the *Theater an der Wien*, and further down a magnificent *Jugendstil Ensemble* (Nos. 38, 40 and

Above: Urban railway station by Otto Wagner on Karlsplatz; behind it, the building of the Musikverein.

Below: Art Hall on Karlsplatz (architect Adolf Krischanitz).

Köstlergasse 3) by Otto Wagner. Directly opposite is another work by the same architect, the Kettenbrückengasse underground station, where the Flea Market begins every Saturday, the meeting point for collectors, connoisseurs and onlookers, the local scene and the local punks.
A tip for those out at night: the market taverns and cafés serve a Wienerschnitzel or a small goulash as early as four o'clock in the morning (except on Sundays).

Spittelberg

"Through this door in the arch, Emperor Joseph II fled" states an inscription inside the Gasthaus "Witwe Bolte". As the history of the building reports, Joseph visited the house incognito in 1778 and, because he apparently behaved "cheekily", was brusquely thrown out of the building. At the time, Spittelberg was the red light district of Vienna, where the "Hübschlerinnen" (the pretty ones) would offer their services by displaying their visible advantages in the windows. Or they would stand in front of the countless taverns using "the arts available to them" to solicit customers. Nowadays these places would be called hostess bars, and how little certain things have changed is shown in the descriptions by the Biedermeier writer Ignaz F. Castelli: "Everything was arranged to swindle the guests to the greatest degree, applying dance, drink and the frivolous caresses of the girls to create in them such a sentiment that they might abandon all caution and empty their purses ..."
"Spittelberg", today a small, hardly noticeable hill from which the Turks, and later Napoleon, directed their guns at Vienna, became an architecturally attractive district during the Baroque period. However, it soon fell into decay again, and the maze of narrow streets attracted craftsmen, day labourers and textile workers, as well as beggars, tramps and the pimps of the numerous prostitutes. Located close to the Imperial

Gate, the most important entry into the city, Spittelberg had enjoyed an international reputation as a district of pleasure since the 18th century: of the 138 houses, 58 were entitled to serve alcoholic drinks. Musicians, popular singers, harp players and whores entertained the public in the taverns and coffee-houses; and there was always a "back room" available for particularly animated guests. These goings-on are the subject of the countless four-line earthy "Spittelberg songs". It is true that the morally strict Empress Maria Theresia attempted to put an end to prostitution and

Christmas market on the Spittelberg.

promiscuity with her "chastity commission", but with only very little success. Right up to the First World War, Spittelberg was one of the most notorious districts of Vienna, and it is due to this that the buildings have all survived to the present.
Over 30 years ago the charm of this district, with its narrow alleys and its old Viennese suburban houses, was suddenly rediscovered. The city began to revitalise it, and today Spittelberg contains an excellently restored unique ensemble of old buildings. At the same time, new life was brought into the attractive Baroque and Biedermeier houses; contemporary apartments were the result, and countless cultural and social initiatives set themselves up. A cultural centre organising musical events, readings, exhibitions and the like was opened in the *Amerlinghaus*, Stiftgasse 8, the birthplace of the Biedermeier painter Friedrich Amerling; there is also a café here with a delightful courtyard. Craft shops, galleries and boutiques moved in and occupied the entire district, their trade further boosted by the craftwork street markets (Saturdays 10.00–18.00 in the warmer sea-

sons, and a Christmas market). Cafés, bars, restaurants and a cinema also bring the district to life in the evening, when guest garden next to guest garden line the romantic car-free alleys in the summer.

Neubau, Josefstadt and Alsergrund

From Spittelberg it is only a stone's throw to St.-Ulrichs-Platz on the other side of Burggasse. Here, the Ulrichskirche (St. Ulrich's Church) is the centre of another picturesque remnant of old Vienna with its 16th–18th century suburban houses. The Burggasse in the direction of the city centre first leads past the officially smallest house in Vienna (on the corner of Burggasse/Breitegasse). This delightful building has a surface area of 14m^2, and houses a clockmaker's workshop and a sales room that resembles a museum of clocks. At the end of Burggasse on the left stands the *Volkstheater*, dating from 1889. This completely new type of theatre was to be a model for the whole of the monarchy: where previously the design had underlined the spectators' differences in rank, this stage was the first to be designed for a middle-class mass public, with fewer boxes and a larger pit that also sloped more to give the back rows a better view.
The Museumsplatz is now to the right, with the former "Trade Fair Palace" (today the *Museum Quarter*). This structure was once the court stables (G. B. Fischer von Erlach, 1721–23) and for a time was home to the Vienna Trade Fair. After years of political disagreement, it has now been converted into a modern Museum Quarter for contemporary interdisciplinary art and cultural activities. Its first occupant was the Vienna Architecture Centre and the "Zoom" Children's Museum, followed by the Museum of Modern Art Ludwig Foundation Vienna, the Leopold Museum (Austria's largest private art collection with works of the Austrian Modern from 1880 to the First World War) and three other museums, artists' studios and an art and events hall. The complex is also home to the *Tabakmuseum*.
Walking from the Museum Quarter along the now busy Museumstrasse towards Josephstadt, it is difficult to imagine that it was here that the aristocracy once had their splendid summer residences constructed outside the city walls: the *Palais Trautson* for instance, designed by J. B. Fischer von Erlach, today the home of the Ministry of Justice. Another example is the Palais Auersperg at the corner of Lerchenfelder Strasse, a magnificent Baroque palace, whose owner from 1721 on, Marchese Capece di Roffrano, is said to have inspired the figure of Octavian in Richard Strauss's opera *Der Rosenkavalier*.
A little further on, Josephstätdter Strasse turns off to the left, with the venerable Café Eiles on the corner to Landesgerichtsstrasse, and opposite it the tavern "Zur Stadt Paris", Heimito von Doderer's favourite abode. The author, who wrote large parts of his novel *Die Dämonen* (The Demons) here, immortalised his regular tavern in the story *Ein anderer Kratki-Baschik*. The establishment has unfortunately now been closed down.
Josefstädterstrasse as at leads outward from the city soon crosses Lange Gasse with its old Viennese suburban houses. To the right is the *Alte Backstube* (Old Bakery), a magnificent Baroque house dating from 1697, whose old sandstone house symbol "The Holy Trinity" can still be seen above the doorway. There was a bakery here from 1701 to 1963 without interruption, and its old furnishings can still be visited. The building also houses a café and a restaurant.
A little further along Josefstädter Strasse is the *Theater in der Josefstadt*, and diagonally opposite, on the corner of Piaristengasse, is the *Alte Löwen Apotheke*, once the most attractive pharmacy in Vienna; Ferdinand Georg Waldmüller painted four works for the entrance, which are now to

be seen in the Austrian Gallery in the Upper Belvedere. In its present form, the entrance is 150 years old. The pharmacy was founded in 1782 and caused a stir in 1816 when its owner was the first to introduce gas lighting in Vienna; this was such a sensation that even the Emperor Franz I came to marvel at it.
The Piaristengasse leads off to the right to *Piaristenplatz* (actually called Jodok-Fink-Platz) with one of the most attractive urban ensembles of Baroque Vienna. The top end of the square is occupied by the *Piaristenkirche* (Church of the Piarists – Maria Treu), by J. L. von Hildebrandt (the attractive ceiling frescos by Franz Anton Maulbertsch are well worth seeing); to the right of the church is a grammar school, to the left the Piarist's college. In the centre of this delightful square is a column to mark the end of the plague. In front of it, in summer, the cafés and taverns put out their tables and chairs, and, against the earnest background of the old monastery walls, you can enjoy purely secular pleasures in an almost Mediterranean atmosphere.
The cellars of the buildings are occupied by the centuries old *Piaristenkeller* with its opulent restaurant. There are both guided tours of the cellar's historic rooms and wine tours with tastings.
A little further on, in Alser Strasse, is the old *Allgemeine Krankenhaus* (General Hospital). To look at the Classicist walls and the complex courtyards, one would not think that this was once the most modern hospital of its age. It created a sensation when it was opened in 1784, and was the subject of many a commentary: "In this hospital, cleanliness is everywhere of the very highest level. Every single patient has a bed of his own ... and when all the rooms are furnished and occupied, around 2000 patients can be admitted."

Palais Auersperg: where Wolfgang Amadeus Mozart and his sister performed.

At the time, the city of Vienna had a population of 250,000, and thus this hospital was one of its most important medical care institutions and the first such major project in the German-speaking world. The adaptation of this complex of buildings, which had previously housed war invalids (from the Turkish siege in 1683), the sick, the poor, children and poor students, for use

The Federal Pathological Anatomical Museum in the "Tower of Fools" of the old General Hospital.

exclusively by sick people, was a first stage on the way towards a modern dedicated hospital. Designed as a teaching hospital from the very start, a hundred years later the now university clinic had become a place of medical pilgrimage, and witnessed the establishment of a new school of medicine. It was thanks to trail-breaking experts such as the pathologist Karl Rokitansky, the specialist in internal medicine Josef Skoda, the surgeons Theodor Billroth and Ferdinand von Hebra, the founder of modern dermatology, that the so-called Second Viennese School of Medicine achieved a world wide reputation. The number of famous Viennese doctors whose achievements were a major contribution to medical progress is legion, and includes the psychiatrist Julius Wagner-Jauregg, Nobel prize winner in 1930. Today these old walls that once housed so many excellent medical pioneers, have a new purpose: a university campus is being established here, while a new huge *General Hospital* (the AKH) has been constructed on Währinger Gürtel after decades of construction work and scandal.
There is however another absolute medical rarity to be marvelled at in the old hospital: the 6th courtyard contains the round *Narrenturm* (Tower of Fools), which, from 1784 on, housed the mad, as they were then known. Emperor Joseph II had forbidden the practice of publicly displaying the mentally ill that had been the rule until then, and ordered that they should henceforward be treated as ill. The tower, popularly called the "Guglhupf" (after a type of cake), is five storeys high, with 139 cells arrange like a prison in order to permit better supervision of the occupants. Today it contains the *Pathological-Anatomical Museum*, a collection founded in 1796. The visit is not for those with weak nerves! The collection contains over 4000 pathological preparations and models, some of which are "parts of the bodies of deceased persons or are surgical specimens from still-living citizens".
The old hospital was built in conjunction with the *Josephinum*, a nearby Classicist building, by Isidor Canevale, who also built the "Narrenturm". Opened in 1785 as the Royal and Imperial Medical-Surgical Military Academy, it was intended to provide the long needed sound training for the "field surgeons" and doctors of the army. The Institute was excellently equipped, and the students were provided with surgical and physical apparatus. In particular, however, Joseph II had 1192 wax anatomical specimens imported from the school of the Italian physiologian Felice Fontana, which are today world-famous. These both realistic and aesthetic models – life-size and in full detail – have been open to the public since the Institute was closed in 1872. The unique collection now belongs to the Institute for the History of Medicine, which is also housed in this building. Other rooms contain a historical student's pharmacy and souvenirs of the great doctors of the Vienna school.
One of these doctors was Sigmund Freud (1856–1939), the founder of psychoanalysis, and it was not far from the

Josephinum that he worked. His home and surgery, today the *Sigmund Freud Museum* and library, is an address known throughout the world: Berggasse 19.
"Between 1900 and 1910, Vienna was the intellectual centre of the world, and Vienna knew nothing about it", wrote the historian Carl Schorske. Few intellectual achievements of the age were so unappreciated as psychoanalysis. Freud was aware of this, and suffered as a result. Nevertheless, it is no accident that it was precisely in turn-of-the-century Vienna that the study of mental illnesses made such great progress. Joie de vivre and morbidity, cosmopolitanism and resentment were seldom so closely bound together as in Vienna. Freud, who studied medicine in Vienna, first worked as a neurologist, at the General Hospital amongst other places; he then turned to hypnosis and psychiatry. The breakthrough to a new understanding of the subconscious came in 1900 with his work *The Interpretation of Dreams*. But the more progress Freud made in his discoveries, attaching a decisive role to sexuality, the more enemies he made. Karl Kraus joked: "It is thanks to him that the anarchy of dreams has been given a constitution. And it's just like in Austria." And Kraus was one of the more reticent. In 1938, the Jewish psychiatrist, now old and sick, was obliged to flee from the Nazis to London, where he died the following year. It is true that Freud had many prominent pupils such as Alfred Adler, C.G. Jung, Wilhelm Reich or Helene Deutsch, but he never obtained a full professorship at the Vienna university. Even after the Second World War it was a struggle for Viennese psychoanalysis to establish itself gradually in academic circles. Freud's monument ended up in a hidden corner in the courtyard of the university. Today, a park near the university may indeed be call the "Sigmund Freud

Sigmund Freud's former surgery, Berggasse 19, is now a museum.

Park", and Freud's face may decorate the 50 Schilling note, but this can hardly disguise the stony path that has led to official recognition of his academic achievements. The Sigmund Freud Museum was opened in 1971, documenting Freud's life and work in the dignified study and treatment rooms. The famous couch, however, is in London. The museum also commemorates Sigmund Freud's daughter, Anna Freud, the eminent child psychoanalyst.

Not far from Berggasse, Liechtensteinstrasse leads to the *Strudlhofstiege* (Strudlhof Stairs), one of the most attractive Jugendstil constructions in Vienna (1910). The broad double stairway leads from Liechtensteinstrasse up to Währinger Strasse. With its fountains, its various levels and the attractive street lamps, it shows – like its Baroque precursors – "more than in words, but also visually, that every track and path is more than a connection between two points, one of which one leaves in order to reach the other ...", as Heimito von Doderer wrote in his novel *Die Strudlhofstiege*, with which he achieved sudden fame in 1951. And vice versa, the success of the book has also made the delightful Strudlhofstiege a popular attraction.

At the foot of the stairs the eye is caught by the Baroque *Palais Liechtenstein*. Domenico Martinelli constructed the garden palace in 1691–1711 at the same time as a town palace for the aristocratic Liechtenstein family, still the owner of the property. The sumptuous building, with a rich decoration of frescos by Johann Michael Rottmayr, Andrea Pozzi and others, was until 1944 home to the Liechtenstein Gallery of Paintings, regarded as the most important private collection in the world until the turn of the century. Since 1979, it has contained part of the *Museum Moderner Kunst Stiftung Ludwig Wien* (Museum of Modern Art, Ludwig Foundation, Vienna).

The Palais Liechtenstein, once the family's city palace, is today a museum of modern art.

From the museum, Porzellangasse leads a little further away from the town centre as far as Seegasse, which contains the oldest surviving Jewish cemetery in the city. First mentioned in documents in 1629, it was the last resting place of many an eminent representative of the Viennese Jewish Community, such as Samuel Oppenheimer and Simon Auerbach. There are over 900 gravestones in Seegasse, the oldest still legible inscription dating from 1582; after the ravages by the Nazis, approximately 280 stones were identified and reerected. It was four decades later, in 1984, that the cemetery, today in the courtyard of an old people's home, was consecrated.

Leopoldstadt

Thanks to its location on the other side of the Danube Canal, Leopoldstadt was always the destination of anyone who arrived from the north and east. It was here that visitors, ambassadors and traders found lodgings before moving on into the city. Immigrants settled here, making Leopoldstadt the most varied and socially mixed district of Vienna. Originally a system of islands exposed to the risk of floods amongst the branches of the Danube, it was the site of the 17th century Jewish ghetto. It later became an important commercial centre, with fishing and shipping and above all trade and transport located here. It was here that the first savings bank was opened in Vienna in

The Jewish cemetery in Seegasse still contains many ancient gravestones.

1819. The carriers, dealers and market goers came from all over the world. Jewish merchants, forbidden before 1848 from living in the city, settled here at its gates, pursuing their business at the tabor or in the coffee-houses along the Danube Canal. In 1837, it was in Leopoldstadt that Salomon von Rothschild constructed the Northern Railway, the first major technical project of the time; The Northern Railway Station, opened in 1864, was the gateway into the imperial capital for the flood of Czech and Jewish immigrants.
In the Vienna of the period before the 1848 revolution, Leopoldstadt was an entertainment quarter of the first order: Johann Strauss (senior) was the bandleader in the Sperl dance hall, while the "Odeon", of which Odeongasse is a reminder, had a capacity of 10,000, and the carriages queued all the way down Praterstrasse.
In addition, Praterstrasse also included the popular Leopolstädter Theatre (subsequently the Carltheater), where Ferdinand Raimund and Johann Nestroy celebrated their successes. Later, with the arrival of the Jewish immigrants, Leopoldstadt became a warren of coffee-houses, a market place for everything: political opinions, goods and all kinds of information. Today things are different; the coffee-house has become rare since the Jews who developed its culture disappeared.
The further one goes from the city, and the closer to the Prater, the more the district is dominated by prostitution, crime and establishments that no guide could ever recommend. Nevertheless, it is not really dangerous here. and in the quiet side alleys with their small shops, often shuttered for ages, there are still find ancient suburban houses and an atmosphere that this is the traditional district of the poor immigrants, small traders, workers and petty criminals.

View over the Danube Canal to the Urania, a traditional centre for popular education.

The "Mazzes Island"

The Ghetto "Im Unteren Werd" represents the second attempt made by the Viennese to concentrate the Jews in a settlement of their own. It was set up in 1625, but scarcely survived two generations; incidents such as the Imperial Palace fire, for which this section of the population was blamed, forced Leopold I to give way to the urgings of the city council and his bigoted wife and to banish the Jews in 1670. From then on, the district was settled by artisans and bore the name "Leopoldstadt".
The Jews were never again to have a district of their own (it was not until the Nazis that the city acquired another ghetto, the starting point for deportations to the concentration camps), and yet this part of Vienna remained closely associated with their history; Jews continued to settle in Leopoldstadt, and in the 19th century the imperial city of Vienna acted like a magnet on the Jews of the cities and schtetls (Jewish villages) of Bohemia, Moravia, Galicia and Hungary. The Jewish middle class moved into the palaces of Praterstrasse, while in the side alleys Jewish dealers, artisans and workers mingled with the other residents. Sigmund Freud, Arthur Schnitzler and Arnold Schönberg grew up on the "Mazzes Island", the name given to the district as a result of its large Jewish population ("Mazze" is the unleavened Passover bread). Veza Canetti (the wife of the Nobel prize winner Elias Canetti) lived here in Ferdinandstrasse, which acquired literary immortality in her moving novel *"Die gelbe Strasse"* (The Yellow Street)
The Jewish community's self confidence was expressed in their religious buildings: Tempelgasse 3–5 was the Large Temple,

the largest synagogue in Vienna, built in 1858 by the Ringstrasse architect Ludwig Förster, who was also the architect of the Large Synagogue in Budapest (the temple was destroyed in 1938, but an old wing still survives; a monument consisting of four columns by Martin Kohlbauer was erected in 1997 in the new wing as a reminder of the former building; there is also a memorial plaque on the Desider-Friedmann-Hof council apartment block). In Zirkusgasse, on the other side of Praterstrasse, the magnificent Turkish Temple of the Sephardic Jews was built in 1887 (and also destroyed in 1938).

The First World War brought with it misery and a new flood of refugees from the east, resulting in a rapid increase in the Jewish population. Half of Vienna's Jews (at its peak, 200,000, or 10% of the population of the city) lived in Leopoldstadt in the 1920s, accounting for 40% of the district's population. The majority were forced into exile or murdered after 1938 and their culture was destroyed. After 1945, it was only gradually that Jewish life re-established itself here, acquiring an additional stimulus through the arrival of Soviet emigrants in the 1970s. Today Leopoldstadt contains prayer houses, schools and clubs (although hardly recognisable from the outside and heavily guarded for security reasons), the "Chaj" bookshop in Lessinggasse, a number of kosher stores and the Jewish-Georgian restaurant "Grusia" at Wolfgang-Schmälzl Gasse 8; in Tempelgasse around the former synagogue, a centre is developing with residential homes, stores, cafés and events' rooms as a place of encounter between Jews and non-Jews – a sign of the vitality of Jewish Vienna in its resistant to the stubborn anti-Semitism and desire to expel them on the part of the Viennese population.

The view across to Leopoldstadt from Schwedenplatz, on the other side of the Danube Canal reveals nothing but a row of high-rise office blocks, with no indication that behind them there still stand ancient houses from the time of the Jewish ghetto. From the Schwedenplatz, the Schwedenbrücke bridge first leads into Taborstrasse, the oldest street in the district, along which since time immemorial hostile armies and peaceful dealers have made their way towards the city. Here is to be found the once so important Agricultural Products Exchange (No. 10), established in 1890 in an attempt to counteract the declining economic significance of this previously so important long-distance road. It is followed by the old *Monastery Church of the Hospitalers* where Joseph Haydn played the organ from 1755 to 1758, and the order's hospital. A little further, diagonally across the road, is the Kirche der *Karmeliter* (Carmelite Church). A left turn leads into the Karmelitergasse, past the Circus and Clown Museum (No. 9) and into the district of the former Ghetto. The Ghetto covered the district between today's Taborstrasse, Obere Augartenstrasse, Malzgasse, Schiffgasse and Krummbaumgasse and included the *Karmelitermarkt*, which opens up at the end of Karmelitergasse, a market with a special atmosphere that recalls the sparkling history of this district (note that the market is only open in the mornings, and at its liveliest on Fridays and Saturdays).

Kosher butchers in the Leopoldstadt.

Inside the Temple in the Tempelgasse. Water-colour by Richard Moser (1922).

Haidgasse leads away from Karmeliterplatz and contains the old Viennese tavern "Zum Sieg" (The Victory), its name deriving from the battle of Aspern in 1809, the first battle that Napoleon lost – and that against the Austrians. The old house symbol that showed the victor, Archduke Karl, was later damaged and replaced in 1978 by the present image above the entrance. The building was first mentioned in 1632, and was originally part of the Ghetto, the property of Israel Liebermann. Grosse Sperlgasse was once the main street and business centre of the district, and still containing some houses from the 17th and 18th centuries. No. 24, the "Seifensiederhaus" (Soap Boiler's house) was built in 1685 on the site of the Jewish Community House, and today contains the *Crime Museum*. The New Synagogue once stood in Grosse Pfarrgasse stood before being pulled down after the liquidation of the ghetto and replaced by the *Leopoldkirche* (St. Leopold's Church).
Otherwise there is little that recalls the ghetto. The Theodor-Herzl-Hof stands on the corner of Malzgasse and Leopoldgasse, a residential block named after the founder of Zionism, but there are hardly any other historical memorials. The Malzgasse leads out of the Jewish Ghetto and suddenly opens out after the narrowness of the old alleys to present a wide panorama from the Spittelau waste incineration plant (designed by Friedensreich Hundertwasser), over the Augarten with its flak towers from the Second World War and the main entrance to the park, and on to the Augarten Palais directly opposite Malzgasse.

From the Augarten to Praterstrasse

Leaving the old ghetto district via Malzgasse, one arrives the *Augarten*, the oldest surviving Baroque garden in Austria, with a monumental system of paths dating back to the 17th century when Emperor Leopold I had the splendid "Favorita" pleasure palace constructed. In 1775 the park was opened to the public as "a place of entertainment dedicated to all people", and soon became one of the social centres of Viennese cultural life. From 1782 on, Mozart, and later Schubert and Beethoven, conducted the so called "Morning Concerts" here. Balls, festivals and competitions were held and from 1820 to 1848 it was here that the popular May 1st concerts took place, with music by Johann Strauss senior. Today the Augarten, like a number of other places in Vienna, is marked by gloomy shadows from the Second World War: two flak towers constructed by the Germans as an air-raid defence in 1940, an immovable presence to which the Viennese have long become accustomed (every attempt to demolish them has failed so far). Around them, the tradition of events in the Augarten is experiencing a new boom: festivals (e.g. the "Festival of the Peoples" in the late summer), concerts and the "Cinema under the Stars", a popular open-air film festival, are amongst the summer attractions.
Since 1922, the gardens have also contained the world famous *Wiener Porzellanmanufaktur Augarten* (Augarten Vienna Porcelain Manufacture). The second oldest porcelain manufacturer in Europe after Meissen, the Vienna Augarten Porcelain Manufacture was founded in 1718 and produces hand-made high-quality tableware in a range of styles from Baroque through Jugenstil to the Modern. Ornaments are also produced, including the famous Lipizzaner models based on originals dating from the time of Maria Theresia – open to view in the sales and

display rooms in the Augarten. The renovated Baroque palace to the right houses another Viennese institution of world repute: the Vienna Boy's Choir, which has been in the Augarten since 1948.
The Augarten was connected to the Prater by a tree-lined boulevard known today as Heinestrasse. It leads directly to the Praterstern, towered over by the *Monument to Vice-Admiral Wilhelm von Tegetthoff* (1827–71), erected in 1886 in memory of Austria's only maritime hero. Today from his lonely height he heroically looks over the multi-lane roundabout at his feet, behind him the Ferris Wheel that marks the entrance to the Volksprater (People's Prater).
One of the seven streets from the Praterstern is *Praterstrasse*, once the "Jägerzeile" (Hunter's row) (until 1862) that linked the city with the Prater. Palace-like buildings are a reminder of the elegant boulevard where, at the end of the 18th century, the aristocracy, followed by financial barons and industrialists, took up residence, and down which the elegant carriages trotted to the Derby or to the coffee-houses in the Prater. Later, the middle classes moved in, including artists, musicians, scholars and doctors. Even when Leopoldstadt had already become an impoverished district, Joseph Roth was still able to write "Praterstrasse is almost aristocratic." It was a colourful and turbulent street with countless shops, hotels, cafés, cabaret theatres and the popular Carltheater.
A curiosity stands close by the Praterstern: the *Dogenhof* (Court of the Doge) in the Venetian style – the sole witness to a plan to construct an Italian quarter here at the end of the 19th century. A plaque on the house next door commemorates the composer Max Steiner, a pioneer of film music, who was born in this house in 1888 and began his career in the theatre and entertainment centre "Venice in Vienna" in the Prater; he later moved to Hollywood, where he became famous by writing the music for *Casablanca* and *Gone with the Wind*. In 1838 the house was converted into the "Hotel Nordbahn", named after the Emperor Ferninand's Northern Railway, which had been opened the year before (today it is a modern elegant hotel with flair). No. 54 commemorates another composer with a world-wide reputation: the apartment of Johann Strauss junior contains a *Museum to the Waltz king* and his famous *Blue Danube Waltz*, which he wrote here in 1867.
A number of impressive religious buildings were also constructed around the once elegant and cheerful Praterstrasse, such as the *Johann Nepomuk Kirche* (St. John Nepomuk Church), an important work of romantic Historicism, followed shortly by the Large Temple in Tempelgasse and the magnificent Turkish Temple of the Sephardic Jews in Zirkusgasse in 1887.
It was in the rear wing of the house "Zum Schwarzen Adler", dating back to 1860, that Alfred Adler, the founder of individual psychology, held his surgery. The wing was actually at Czerningasse 7, but Adler preferred the "more elegant address" of Praterstrasse 44.
No. 31 is the site of the Carltheater mentioned above, constructed in 1848 as the successor to the legendary Leopoldstädter Theater, and where Franz von Suppé's first operettas were performed. Johann Nestroy was the dramatist in residence, stage star and, from 1854, director of the theatre. It was closed in 1929, and pulled down in 1951 as a bombed ruin. Today the site is occupied by the "Galaxie" office block.
Nestroy is commemorated by the square named after him and by a monument at Praterstrasse 19, now the small café restaurant "Zum Mahder – Am Platzl" and an appropriate spot to finish this tour. The first storey of this late Classicist building with a view of the top of the "Steffl" tower in the inner city contains a cannon ball bearing the date 1809, a memorial of the battle against Napoleon at the gates of Vienna. Praterstrasse 16 was where the doc-

tor and dramatist Arthur Schnitzler was born in 1862, while in 1924, the writer and Nobel prize winner Elias Canetti moved into a room at No. 22 to begin his chemistry studies in Vienna. His existence here was very modest, and he claims he only saw it through because his landlady brought him a generous breakfast every day.

The Prater

The Prater, another prominent part of Leopoldstadt, is *the* entertainment and relaxation area of Vienna. A vast expanse surrounded by buildings and streets, it contains not only the Volksprater (People's Prater, amusement park) but also an area of forest and riverside meadows. From 1560, it was the hunting property of the Habsburgs, but was opened to the public by Joseph II in 1766. It was immediately stormed by the Viennese, and soon refreshment tents, puppet theatres, fairground stands, bowling alleys, roundabouts, swings and taverns under the old trees had created the *Wurstelprater* (deriving from the figure of Hanswurst (harlequin); officially the Volksprater), while families went walking, lovers met and enemies duelled in the broad expanses of the riverside meadows. The Prater was from the very start not simply a place of amusement but also of pleasures and vice. The three elegant coffee-houses along the main avenue were always crowded, and still today bets are placed on the horses at the Race courses at the *Krieau* (trotting races) and the *Freudenau* (gallop). Today the Volksprater is a huge amusement park with a special Viennese atmosphere, and is shortly to be expanded; during the day it is an entertainment for old and young, at night somewhat more dubious. And above all the entertainments and the fragrant reminiscences of the imperial and royal era, from the Burenwurst (hot sausage) to čevapčiči and from langos (sausage in batter) to turkish delight, stands the Riesenrad (Ferris Wheel), constructed in 1897 and a technical masterpiece of Bri-

The People's or "Wurstel" Prater, Vienna's popular amusement park.

View over the city from a car of the Ferris Wheel.

tish engineering. One of the key scenes in Orson Welles' film *The Third Man* was set in one of the red cars of this wheel, making this Viennese landmark instantly famous around the world. It was constructed in 1897 by the English engineer Walter B. Basset on the occasion of Emperor Franz Joseph's Golden Jubilee. It weights 440 tonnes, is 64.7 m high, with 120 spokes and 15 cars (originally 30) and turns exactly in a north-south direction.

A comfortable way of exploring the large areas of the Prater is a ride on the miniature railway from the Ferris Wheel to the Heustadelwasser; having arrived at this remnant of one of the once many arms of the Danube, you can take a ride in a boat or cool your feet. The huge Prater area

Freudenau race track.

contains not only the Volksprater but also an exhibition centre, sports stadiums, a public swimming pool, numerous sports grounds and meadows such as the popular Jesuitenwiese (Jesuits' Meadow), where whole families picnic and individuals enjoy the sun or read the newspaper; there are countless playgrounds for children.

The Hauptallee (Main Avenue) is a 4.5 km long paradise for joggers, cyclists, riders, dogs and walkers. It leads in a straight line to the *Lusthaus*, an attractive eight-sided Baroque pavilion, built by the river in 1784, originally a small castle for imperial hunting groups and the venue for magnificent festivities. Since the end of the monarchy, the Lusthaus has been a café restaurant. Diagonally opposite is the popular restaurant "Altes Jägerhaus". From here it is not far to the gallop race course in the Freudenau, which dates back to the second half of the 19th century when the Prater was still the second stop of an upper-middle-class Sunday after the promenade on Kärntner Ring.

Mexikoplatz – bazaar on the Danube

The wide expanse of Mexikoplatz is to be found at the point where Lassallestrasse

meets the Danube, dominated by the unusual Church of St. Francis of Assisi (also called the Jubilee Church) constructed on the occasion of Emperor Franz Joseph's Golden Jubilee (1898). After the assassination of the Empress in the same year, the Empress *Elisabeth Memorial Chapel* was added to the left transept.
From Mexikoplatz, the *Reichsbrücke* crosses the Danube to Floridsdorf. It was here that in April 1945 the retreating German troops fled to the left bank of the Danube (after the war the bridge was called the bridge of the Red Army). The only bridge to survive all the battles intact, it suddenly collapsed in August 1976 and had to be rebuilt.
But why is it called Mexikoplatz? Is it intended as a memory to Maximilian, the brother of Franz Joseph shot in Mexico in 1867? Or is it an expression of thanks to Mexico, which was the only country to refuse to grant diplomatic recognition of Austria's Anschluss with Germany in 1938, as a plaque on the square announces? Whatever it may be, life in "Mexiko", as the area around the square is popularly known, has less to do with the far west than with the near east. Before the opening of the borders of eastern Europe, the square was the destination for cut-price tourists from Poland, Soviet bargees and all kinds of lost souls from Bulgaria or Rumania; in the meantime police raids against smugglers and the political upheavals of the east have changed the legendary bazaar character of this district. But you can still feel it: the countless small stores still present a colourful confusion and unbelievable choice of inexpensive watches, pocket calculators, textiles, chewing gum, camp beds and vodka, the stores still bear Slav or eastern Jewish names, and the mixture of languages is the background music to the fates, longings and hopes of the immigrants – just as it has always been in this district of immigrants and the stateless.

The Reichsbrücke and – in the background – the church of St. Francis of Assisi on Mexikoplatz.

Between the Gürtel and the Vienna Woods

Although Vienna is a large city, its dimensions remain manageable and clearly structured: the historical centre, the inner city, is contained by the Ringstrasse, where once stood the old city walls. The former suburbs (today the 3rd to the 9th Districts) form a semi-circle round the Ring, and the 2nd and 20th districts are between the Danube Canal and the Danube River. Roughly where the former so-called line rampart ran, a second ring of defence built by Prince Eugene in 1704, lies the Gürtel, a four-lane road and notorious red light district, the subject of attempts at urban renewal and revival by architects, city planners and artists – with the assistance of EU subsidies. And beyond the Gürtel extend the former "Vororte", Vienna's outer districts (10th–19th Districts) forming a wide circle around the city. Here, in the traditional working districts of Favoriten and Ottakring, for instance, high, dust-grey 19th century apartment houses line the streets, inhabited today by Viennese, guest-workers and immigrants, a coexistence that is by no means free from friction. In contrast, Hietzing, Währing and Döbling are the elegant and exclusive districts of mansions and villas. Tourists rarely stray into these "Vororte", nor are they a frequent sight in the districts of Floridsdorf and Donaustadt (21st and 22nd Districts) across the Danube, except for a visit to a Heurige. But in fact it is well worth exploring these districts, the home of the Viennese and the immigrants, with their contrasts in attitude and social status, particularly since the outer districts contain a number of highlights which themselves make the journey worth while.

Schönbrunn Palace and Park.

Schönbrunn Palace and Park

After the glorious victory over the Turks, Emperor Leopold I commissioned J. B. Fischer von Erlach to build an imperial pleasure palace on the site of an old and now destroyed hunting castle. Fischer's ambitious plan provided for a castle on the Gloriette hill that was to outdo Versailles

in magnificence; however, the imperial house, notoriously short of money, lacked the funds for such grandeur. The "more modest" alternative with 1,441 rooms and halls was created between 1669 and 1730. From 1744 to 1749, the complex was redesigned by Nicolaus Pacassi as a residence for Maria Theresia, and, with the exception of a number of changes from 1816 to 1819, it is in this form that it can be seen today. The restoration after the major damage caused by the Second World War was completed in 1952.
After the death of Maria Theresia, the Baroque Schönbrunn experienced its heyday during the Congress of Vienna, which met here in 1814/15. And it was in Schönbrunn that the Monarchy came to an end

View over Schönbrunn Palace to the Gloriette.

in 1918 when Karl I signed his abdication in the Blue Salon and Austria became a republic. It has also been used as a billet on several occasions: in 1805 and 1809, when his troops occupied Vienna, Napoleon I lodged in Maria Theresia's favourite rooms; and his sickly son, the Duke of Reichstadt, lived here until his early death in 1832. In 1945, the British High Commissioner established his headquarters in the Palace. Today the Habsburg's former summer residence, operated as a private enterprise since 1992, is used as the sumptuous setting for state receptions.

The "Wagenburg" in Schönbrunn contains a collection of historic state and utility carriages.

39 rooms, a fraction of the Palace's total, can be visited, and provide an insight into the imperial domestic style. The Porcelain Room, the Miniature's Cabinet and the Writing Room are examples of the zenith of the Rococo. The chinoiseries in many of the rooms show that Asia was in fashion amongst the aristocracy – but in Vienna, as so often, with a slight delay. And it was in the Hall of Mirrors, usually used for swearing in ministers, that the six-year-old prodigy Mozart gave his legendary concert before Maria Theresia in 1762. The other state rooms include the Million Gulden Room with its 260 Indian parchment miniatures, the Napoleon Room with its Brussels tapestries and the Large Gallery – the splendid festival hall in the centre of the palace.

The large *Palace Park* is one of the world's most important Baroque gardens and plenty of time should be allowed to discover it. There are two entrances to the park. The entry from the Hietzing Gate (Hietzing U4 underground station) first passes the imposing *Palm House*, the largest greenhouse in Europe, dating back to the Ringstrasse era, with the *Butterfly House* immediately adjoining. A little further comes the *Tiergarten* (Zoo). In this, the oldest zoo in the world, there are still a number of Baroque enclosures standing and, in the middle, the Emperor's Breakfast Pavilion. In this Pavillion (today a café) a Baroque fresco was found that had twice been painted over. It was uncovered in March 1998. Further along, the path suddenly opens up to give a breathtaking view of the Palace and the huge carpet of flowers in front of it, with a formal avenue of statues inspired by Antiquity leading up to the entrance.

The climb to the *Gloriette* along the zigzag path from the *Neptune Fountains* is an absolute must. The view over Vienna and the majestic Palace in its shining "Schönbrunn yellow", the model for countless palaces, villas and middle class houses during the Monarchy, is really worth the effort. There is a further attraction in the form of a delightful café installed in the previously open-sided Gloriette. It is on the same level as the *Tyrolean Garden* with an alpine-style tavern inspired by the Romanticism of nature in fashion at the time. On the side of the park towards the Meidling Gate (Schönbrunn U4 underground station), at the same level as the Neptune fountain, there are *Roman Ruins* to explore. Constructed in 1778 as a romantic ruin, they testify to the age's admiration for everything antique. Not far away is the *Schöner Brunnen* (Beautiful Fountain) that gave its name to the Palace as a whole, the *Obelisk*, and, in a delightful location, the old Viennese Schönbrunn Café Meierei in the Kronprinzengarten (Garden of the Crown Prince) hidden behind a maze of hedges.

Not part of the palace park, but located within its grounds, is the *Hietzinger Fried-*

View from the Schönbrunn Palace Park to the Gloriette.

hof (Hietzing Cemetery), where the contrast with middle class ostentation is well worth seeing. Its representative mausoleums and temple constructions are proof that, even in death, some are more noble than others. Among its residents are Franz Grillparzer (1872), the popular dancer Fanny Elssler (1884), the architect Otto Wagner (1918), the Jugenstil artists Gustav Klimt (1918) and Kolo Moser (1918), the composer Alban Berg (1935) and the actress Katharina Schratt (1940), better known to posterity as the mistress of Emperor Franz Joseph.

Der Zentralfriedhof (the Central Cemetery)

The Viennese are said to have a special relationship with death, and rightly so. Dying may be no easier to bear here than anywhere else, but the Viennese uniquely decorate and embellish what they are afraid of. Is the "Schöne Leich" (beautiful corpse), i.e. the extravagant funeral, frivolous or a pompous metaphor for the appetite for the transient? Whatever the answer, the Viennese funeral cult reaches its perfect culmination at the Zentralfriedhof (Central Cemetery). This famous burial ground, the largest in Vienna, contains over 300,000 graves in an area of 2.5 km^2 – and its almost 3 million residents make the city of the dead far more populous than the Vienna of the living. It is here that are revealed essential aspects of the Viennese world of emotions, between endless – at times morbidly sumptuous – rows of graves and the life associated with it: people out for a stroll or watering flowers, the devout, the curious, those seeking contact. The flower shop, stonemasons, taverns and sausage stands at the gates. And on All Saints' Day (November 1st), hundreds of thousands of Viennese make their way to the cemetery

Honorary grave at the Central Cemetery.

with flowers and candles in pilgrimage to their dead. It was not without reason that the Viennese used to say that the Central Cemetery was half as big but twice as much fun as Zurich. In addition to the deeper understanding of the Viennese mentality, the Central Cemetery of course also contains things of cultural and historical interest. Opened in 1874, the *monumental Main Entrance* (Gate 2) was designed by Max Hegele in 1905. This Jugendstil architect also constructed the massive *Karl Lueger Church* in the centre of the cemetery in 1907–10, a counterpoint to Otto Wagner's Jugenstil Church am Steinhof. From the main entrance an avenue leads to the *Graves of Honour*, the final resting place of all the notables of Vienna. The long neglected *Israelitische Abteilung* (Jewish Section) also contains memorials to the great: Karl Kraus, Arthur Schnitzler, Friedrich Torberg and many others are buried here. There is also a new Jewish section (Gate 5), a Protestant section (Gate 3) and a Russian Orthodox section (Gate 2), and separate sections for the victims of the 1848 revolution, the two World Wars and the Jewish dead of the First World War.
On the other side of the Simmeringer Hauptstrasse, opposite the main entrance, the grounds of the "Neugebäude" Renaissance palace contain the *Crematorium* constructed by Clemens Holzmeister in 1922, and the urn cemetery.

The Karl Marx Hof

It was according to the motto "light in the apartment – sun in the heart" that Red Vienna constructed the "Gemeindebauten", huge city-owned residential complexes built to the then latest standards of construction and health and intended to replace the dark, musty and overcrowded small apartments in the apartment blocks of the working districts. One of the most famous of these complexes is the *Karl Marx Hof* in Heiligenstadt, completed in only three years by Karl Ehn, a pupil of Otto Wagner. The gigantic block with its prominent towers covers an area of 156,000 m^2,

Symbol of "Red Vienna": the Karl Marx Hof.

of which only 18.4% consists of buildings, with the result that numerous grassy courtyards brought light and air into the resident's lives. A previously unknown level of infrastructure provided the total of 1,388 apartments with laundries, kindergartens, a children's dental clinic, a youth centre, a library and swimming pools, as well as a post office, a pharmacy, an outpatients clinic and countless shops.
The Karl Marx Hof is thus a triumph of the social residential construction policy of the Social Democratic city administration, which created a total of 400 worker settlements in the 1920s and the 1930s. They were to be "fortresses of the people", as Otto Glöckel, the great educational reformer, enthused in his opening speech in 1930, a challenge by the proletariat to its previous oppressors, who were held responsible for the poverty and misery of the population. Strongholds of the labour movement, these council complexes certainly were. In the February 1934 uprising, they were the centres of the armed conflict, during which not only the Karl Marx Hof came under heavy fire. The total number of casualties among the "Schutzbund" worker militia was estimated at between 1,500 and 2,000, but victory went to Austro-Fascism. Not only the reform policies of the Social Democrats, of which the Karl Marx Hof is a visible symbol, but all the worker parties and organisations were banned during the following eleven years of dictatorship.

The Wotruba Church

At almost the other end of the city, on the Georgenberg in the Mauer district, there is a monument of a completely different kind that is well worth seeing: the Church *Zur Heiligsten Dreifaltigkeit* (The Most Holy Trinity), usually called the Wotruba Church after its designer. Completed in 1976 according to plans by Fritz Wotruba (1907–75), one of Austria's most prominent sculptors, the unusual building stands on a small hill and is visible for miles around. Transcending the distinctions between architecture and sculpture, the extraordinary church had already been the subject of vehement controversy before it was completed, and has become a destination not only for the curious faithful, but also for art-lovers and architects. The church, designed as layers of stone blocks, was intended by Wotruba to be an invitation to meditation, not a building and not a "container", not a hall, not a central construction but a symbol occupying space, a dynamic interplay of forces. Wotruba's ideas embody the sculptor's three-dimensional style, and were executed after his death by the architect Fritz Mayr. The building is made up of 152 smooth concrete cubes of almost archaic appearance, combined with glass surfaces, some of which were only included during the construction stage. The church manages without opulent furnishings and religious symbols of power, and its only decoration is a crucifix inside. The artist, who did not live to see the completion of his work, wanted to show "that harmony can only be achieved by overcoming a multitude of opposites".

The church on the Georgenberg, built to a design by the sculptor Fritz Wotruba.

Into the Country – Vienna and its Surroundings

The *Kahlenberg* (484 m) is the most popular of the hills around Vienna. On clear days there is a view over the city and the Danube as far as the Schneeberg mountains and the Small Carpathians. Historically there has been a certain amount of confusion: it is claimed that the papal legate, Marco d'Aviano, and the Polish King Jan Sobieski celebrated mass here in 1683 before Sobieski led his relief army down the hill to free Vienna from the Turkish siege. The Baroque *Church of St. Joseph*, full of kitsch and votive offerings, is today run by Poles and the Sobieski Chapel inside it is a popular national Polish shrine. However, it is now pretty certain that the historic mass was held on the neighbouring *Leopoldsberg* (425 m). And to confuse things even more, there has also been a change of names: originally, the Kahlenberg was called the Sauberg thanks to its plentiful wild boar ("Sau"), and the Leopoldsberg was called the Kahlenberg. But when the Church of St. Leopold was built on what is today the Leopoldsberg in 1693, the hills simply changed names.

Many of the trees in the Vienna Woods bear such testimony to past "creativity".

The Kahlenberg with its self service restaurant and large terrace is a popular tourist attraction, particularly at weekends. It is somewhat quieter on the Leopoldsberg with its attractive church, information panels about the Turkish siege of Vienna and the ruins of the old Babenberg fortifications (1135), as well as an equally excellent view.

In addition to its local hills, another destination for a trip out of town is the Vienna Woods *(Wienerwald)*, a unique landscape of forests and meadows forming a

semi-circle round the city, from the Danube valley in the north via the alpine foothills to the west and as far as the Piesting and Triesting valleys in the south. The Vienna Woods are Vienna's green lung, with countless places to stop, ponds, view-points, meadows, taverns, toboggan runs and even skiing areas – and all accessible by public transport.

One of the most attractive destinations in the Vienna Woods is the *Lainz Animal Reserve*, a 25 km^2 nature reserve with 80 km of picturesque paths through ancient oak and beech forests and a large stock of game, including deer, stags, mouflons, aurochs, wild horses and around

Hay transport in the Vienna Woods.

1,000 wild boar. The main attraction is the *Hermes Villa* by the Lainz Gate, constructed by Emperor Franz Joseph for his wife Elisabeth in 1882. There are always attractive year-long exhibitions of interest for the whole family.
Vienna's number one leisure paradise is today the area of the *New Danube*. The Danube at Vienna, by no means as blue as the famous waltz might make us think, is today split by the *Danube Island*. Built in the 1970s as a means of flood prevention, it has become the largest and most popular leisure area of the Viennese: over 40 km of bathing beaches, countless restaurants and leisure facilities, barbecue spots and all kinds of sports and games from surfing, sailing, diving, boating, through cycling and inline skating to the 30-metre-long water-slide (at the Copa Cagrana). While the north and south parts of the island have been generally left unspoiled, the central part has been architecturally designed. Here, not far from the Reichsbrücke (U1 Donauinsel underground station), is the popular *Copa Cagrana* (named after the nearby district of Kagran), by day a bathing beach easily reached and hence crowded to bursting point, by night a popular amusement area with countless restaurants, bars and floating discos – a colourful mixture of every

source of fun – and above it a starry sky that costs nothing at all. Every year in early spring it is also the venue for the extremely popular three-day Danube Island Festival.
The *Lobau* begins south of the island. This 2,500 hectare original riverside meadow area is still within the city limits. A wilderness with a unique world of flora and fauna, a traditional centre of naturalism, a local recreation area for city dwellers, a paradise for outsiders and alternative cultures – this has always been the Lobau. A reminder that this is historic soil is to be found in the Napoleon Stone, a small obelisk bearing the inscription

There's a lot going on on the Danube island on summer evenings.

"Napoleon 1809". It was here that the Corsican set up camp, it was from here that he planned to attack Vienna and it was here that he suffered his first defeat. The Prater and the Lobau have always been the absolute embodiment of riverside meadows for the Viennese. Since environmentalists occupied the riverside meadows near Hainburg in order to save this landscape in 1984, the concept has expanded. The informed tourist today knows that there are a total of 10,000 hectares of intact riverside meadow landscape to the east of Vienna that enjoy protection as a national park.
The Danube by Vienna used to be broken up into a network of branches rich in fish and a regular cause of devastating floods. For this reason, a major regulation of the Danube was carried out from 1868 to 1881, with technical methods that had been successful during the construction of the Suez Canal being used to force the river into a single bed. The result was an unattractive straight river and an equally unattractive flood area. The branch of the river on which Vienna actually lay became what is today the Danube Canal, no longer usable by Danube shipping. Another arm of the original Danube became a 1.6 km^2 stretch of standing water: the *Old Danube*, a classic Viennese recreation area, and a worker culture paradise of Red Vienna. The traces of the past remain alive today.

Schneider boat hire on the Old Danube.

The area boasts wide expanses of allotments, traditional taverns, numerous rowing and sports associations and tranquil bathing beaches. The oldest and largest bathing area is the still popular *Gänsehäufel* (built in 1900), with its countless beaches, swimming pools, restaurants, cabins and a nudist area. North of it, past the old Kaiserwasser with its beaches and boat hire businesses, is the *Danube Park*, created in 1964 as the venue for the Vienna International Gardening Exhibition, and later opened to the public. This huge open space contains sports facilities, playgrounds, cycle tracks, a crazy golf course, taverns and much more. To get an overview, it is worth while taking a tour on the miniature railway or, even more comfortably, taking the chair-lift that sways high above the park. The ultimate highlight is the 252 m high Danube Tower, with its two revolving café-restaurants 160 and 170 m up in the air, both providing a magnificent panorama; at a height of 150 m, there is a panorama terrace open to the public.

Vienna Special

In the Footsteps of "Sisi" and Franz Joseph I

On April 23rd, 1879, Vienna was witness to the imperial silver wedding anniversary. The people flooded into the city and lined the streets to pay tribute to the couple. Unfortunately, it was raining, and the main attraction, the large "historical and illustrated parade" put on by the citizens of Vienna for the happy couple, had to be postponed until April 27th. It involved 14,000 people in historical costumes, representing trade, industry, craft, commerce, the railways, the fine arts and folklore. The parade took two hours to pass the two hundred and thirty thousand spectators and the imperial couple on the recently opened Ringstrasse. There were groups on horseback, fanfares, magnificent coaches and costumes, while, to the cheers of the crowds, the fine arts section was led by the painter Hans Makart, the organiser of the whole event. Emperor Franz Joseph watched the whole thing standing, and was, according to the press, "deeply moved". The Empress was also said to be "deeply moved" – which is highly improbable. She confessed to her lady-in-waiting and niece Maria Wallersee that twenty-five years of marriage had been enough, and it was utterly superfluous to organise a festivity for the occasion. At that time Empress Elisabeth I, nicknamed "Sisi", was forty-one years old and already "the most beautiful grandmother" in the country. Her husband was forty-eight and the couple had long grown apart. Yet everything had begun so magically. Elisabeth (1837–98) came from the Wittelsbach family, which had also produced eccentrics like her cousin, King Ludwig II of Bavaria. Her childhood had been independent and free of care and she was still very young when she unexpectedly met Franz Joseph I (1830–1916), another cousin, in Bad Ischl. For two days, the young Emperor courted her, despite already being promised to her sister, Helene. Upsetting all his mothers plans, they became engaged when Elisabeth was fifteen years old and married nine months later in Vienna. The fairy-tale wedding of the century was staged with huge pomp and circumstance, starting with a journey by rose-decorated paddle-steamer down the Danube to Vienna, to the enthusiastic cheers of the crowd, followed by a reception given by the Habsburgs in Schönbrunn Palace and ending with the Emperor's bride's formal entrance into the city in a state carriage pulled by eight Lipizzaners. Vienna lay at Sisi's feet. At seven o'clock in the evening on April 24th, 1854, the couple were married in the Augustinerkirche, after which the ceremonial parade drove to the Imperial Court where a long programme of audiences awaited the exhausted Elisabeth.

Violin with portrait of Emperor Franz Joseph.

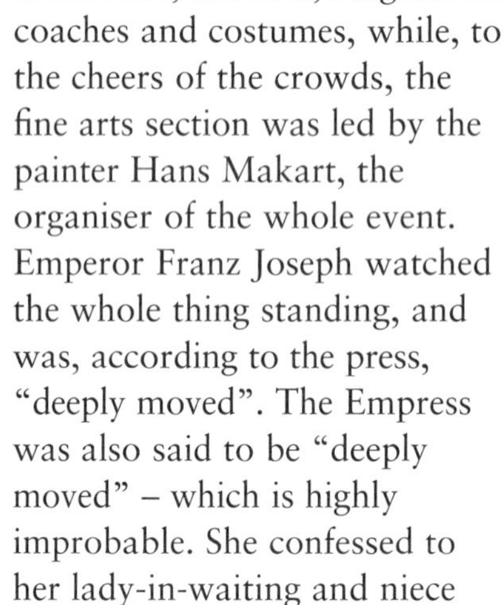

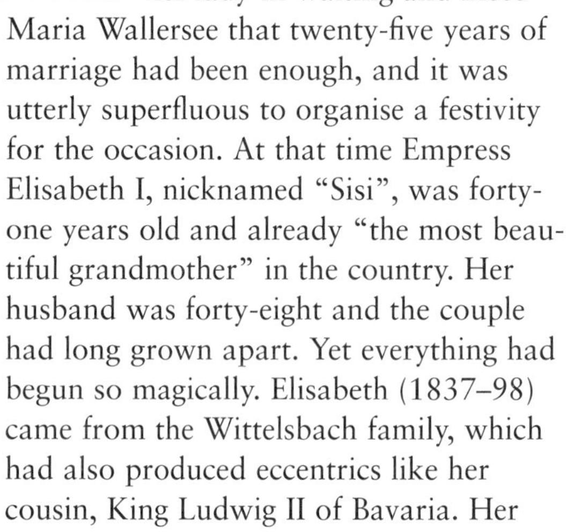

The couple spent their honeymoon in the imperial summer residence of Laxenburg, 15 km south of Vienna. Then everyday life began; Franz Joseph went about his business, while his mother Sophie put into practice her severe re-education programme designed to turn the Bavarian girl into a worthy Habsburg Empress, a task she was never to complete to perfection. Elisabeth hated Sophie, hated the rigid ceremonies of the Habsburg court, its obligations and formalities, and its court society, and found little consolation with her husband, who loved her but had a total lack of sympathetic understanding. She became pregnant. In 1855 her daughter Sophie was born, in 1856 Gisela, and in 1858 the long await-ed crown prince Rudolf. Thus the Empress had done her duty. She was not particularly fond of Gisela and Rudolf, (Sophie died at the age of two, and the youngest adored daughter Marie Valerie

was not born until 1868), particularly since her mother-in-law immediately took on responsibility for the education of the children. In the war against France and Italy, Franz Joseph was far less successful in military matters than in affairs of the heart, as his wife was appalled to find. Sisi withdrew from the Court and from the Emperor, performing only the most necessary official duties, and often not even that, devoting herself and all her passions to the beauty of her slim body, riding and her dogs, and travelling as often as possible. The marriage had collapsed.
The Viennese may gradually have come to moan about their capricious, ever-absent Empress, but the tragedy of Mayerling won her back their sympathy. In this imperial hunting palace near Vienna, for reasons that are still not entirely clear, her only son Rudolf shot his mistress and then himself and though Sisi had never particularly loved him, she was so inconsolable that she spent the rest of her life wearing black. With age, Elisabeth's health became weaker, not least because of her obsessive crash-diets, but her death was to be a violent one; in 1898, on one of her trips abroad, she was stabbed with a file by the Italian anarchist Luigi Lucheni in Geneva.
The parallels to the fate of Princess Diana are unavoidable. The fairy-tale marriage of the young "innocent" girl with a man she hardly knew. Then finding herself suddenly in a central social position with alluring advantages but unbearable disadvantages. A marriage that rapidly became a disaster, overshadowed by the coldness of the court. And two couples who divide historians and public opinion. Was *he* an insensitive pedant who had already begun cheating on his wife during their honeymoon? Or was *she* an exalted neurotic with her mind on nothing more than her appearance? Whatever the answer, both, Diana and Elisabeth, conquered the hearts of their people and their beauty and their tragedy has turned them into a myth far beyond their historical importance. In the case of the Empress, a further important contributing factor was the *Sissi* films in the 1950s, bringing Romi Schneider (another cult figure) her first fame. The musical *Elisabeth*, launched in 1992 and only ending its run in April 1998, was the most successful German-speaking production of all times.
Emperor Franz Joseph I survived his wife by almost two decades. He remained a widower, consoling himself with the already existing liaison with the National

Imperial apartments in the Imperial Palace, in the background the statue of Empress Elisabeth by Herman Klotz.

The Maria Theresia apartments in the Imperial Palace.

Theatre actress Katharina Schratt. He had ascended the throne at the age of eighteen, at the instigation of his ambitious mother in the year of revolution 1848, and his sixty-eight years of reign made him the longest-serving Austrian monarch. It was under his rule that the collapse of the huge multi-ethnic state began. "I am not spared anything ..." was one of the famous standard phrases of the legendary monarch. He died in Schönbrunn in 1916 in the middle of the First World War. His tomb is in the Kapuzinergruft (Imperial burial vault) between his wife's and his son's. His great-nephew Carl ruled for two years and was then obliged to abdicate and leave the country. The monarchy was irrevocably over.

Imperial Vienna

"Sisi" Monument in the Volksgarten. Beauty for eternity. In the most northern corner of the Volksgarten, one of the most beautiful Secessionist monuments is a memorial to the Empress Elisabeth. It was erected by public subscription in 1907 after her murder. The sculptor was Hans Bitterlich, while the attractive semi-circular balustrade was designed by Friedrich Ohmann. On a marble pedestal stands a melancholic "Sisi", agelessly young, the rear of the pedestal bearing the inscription; "The Peoples of Austria erected this monument to their unforgettable Empress Elisabeth in steadfast love and loyalty." A quiet, meditative spot, a place to reflect.

Franz Joseph Monument in the Burggarten. No monuments were erected while the monarch was still alive, an amazing fact in the light of the huge trade in souvenirs at the time. And the First Republic which followed the monarchy felt no need for one. It was only in 1957 that this statue of a rather distant monarch in military uniform was brought to Vienna from Wiener Neustadt as a result of a private initiative, and erected at this somewhat concealed spot.

Hofburg. The Imperial Palace in the centre of Vienna was the residence of the Austrian monarchs for over 600 years and the seat of the Holy Roman Emperor for the two and a half centuries before 1806. It was from this European centre of power that the Habsburgs ruled their multi-ethnic state. Even today the Imperial Palace is the official residence of the Austrian head of state. The Federal President carries out his office and represents the country in the same state rooms as Maria Theresia or Franz Joseph before him, and it is for this reason that these rooms are not open to the general public. Instead, it is possible to see the Habsburg treasures and the Imperial Apartments within this huge complex of buildings.

The Display Rooms of the Hofburg (Imperial Apartments) include the *Franz Joseph apartments* in the Reichskanzleitrakt (Imperial Chancellery Wing) and Elisabeth's rooms in the Amalientrakt (Amalia Wing). The finely furnished Franz Joseph Apartments include the *dining room*, where the Emperor feasted with his officers, conversing with them afterwards around the rococo tiled stove in the *Cercle Room*, or in the *Smoking Room*. It was in the *Large Audience Hall* that the visitors waited beneath the Bohemian crystal chandelier to be received at the twice-

Dining room with the Imperial Court Service in the Imperial Apartments.

weekly audiences of their majesties in the *Audience Room* (the writing stand bears an audience list dated January 3rd, 1910). It is reported that the audiences took place standing, with the Emperor standing next to the writing stand. Consultations with the Council of Ministers and the Crown Council took place in the *Conference Room* with its Empire furnishings. The *Work Room*, furnished in rosewood, is in the style of Louis XV. In contrast, the *Bedchamber* appears modest. Franz Joseph was personally undemanding, sleeping on a simple iron bed and taking his bath in a wooden tub set up in the bedroom. The highlight of the room is the famous painting by Franz Xaver Winterhalter showing the Empress Elisabeth in a long robe and with the star ornament in her untied hair. The **Elisabeth Apartments** include one of the most attractive rooms in the Imperial Palace: the Empress's *living room and bedroom* with a writing desk, lectern, a neo-gothic private altar made of Carraro marble and a Spartan iron bed that was removed during the day. A sensation for the age was the *gymnastics room* that the diet-fanatic had had installed in her toilet room, zealously using it to the displeasure of the Court. The *Large Salon* is splendidly appointed, from the Louis XIV furniture to the works of art. The *small salon* contains souvenirs of the Empress including a photograph of the dress she was wearing on the day of the assassination. The **Alexander Apartments**, named after Tsar Alexander I, who lived here during the Congress of Vienna, include the *Crown Prince Rudolf Memorial Room*, showing a photograph of the unfortunate son of Elisabeth and Franz Joseph; two paintings portray his wife Stephanie and Archduke

Imperial Palace, Imperial Tableware and Silver Chamber, display with table porcelain.

Franz Ferdinand. The *Dining Room* contains a sumptuosly set "supreme imperial table"; all the cutlery is to the right of the plate in accordance with Spanish court etiquette.

The Imperial Silver And Tableware Chamber, reopened in 1995 after conversion and restoration, displays the ceremonial and everyday tableware of the Imperial Court, including Franz Joseph's table linen, as well as valuable eastern Asian porcelain, the gala service from the time of Emperor Franz Joseph, which is still used today at state receptions, Viennese and Parisian silver cutlery, the "English service" (a gift from Queen Victoria to Emperor Franz Joseph), and much more.

The non-plus-ultra in the Imperial Palace is the **Secular and Sacred Treasury**. Reopened in 1987 after four years of reconstruction work, the twenty-one rooms display the imperial treasures and relics of the Holy Roman Empire, coronation and knightly insignias, national emblems, countless secular and ecclesiastical treasures as well as ornaments and souvenirs of inestimable value from the Habsburg possessions.

State Room of the National Library. The Austrian National Library once contained the precious collection of books of the Supreme Imperial Court. The rich collections date back to the 14th century, and were transferred to state ownership in 1920. The first Imperial Library Director was appointed in the 16th century. Today there are roughly 2.5 million books plus the following independent collections: printed materials, manuscripts, maps and globe, papyrus, portrait/picture archive, music and theatre collection and the Esperanto Museum. You should not miss the high-Baroque State Room, today used for exhibitions. The magnificent oval, two-storey room (built by Fischer von Erlach father and son from 1723–1726), is crowned by a mighty cupola with ceiling frescos by Daniel Gran in honour of Karl VI; the marble, life-size statues of emperors were made by Paul and Peter Strudel around 1700. In the middle of this, no doubt the most beautiful library room in the world, stand the precious sixteen thousand gold-embossed volumes of the former library of Prince of Savoy.

Spanish Riding School. Also part of the Imperial Palace and accessible from the Josefsplatz, the Winter Riding School is where prominent guests have always been honoured with a performance by the Spanish Riding School. The famous snow-white Lipizzaners originated from Lipizza in the Krain Karst (Slovenia), where an imperial stud-farm was founded in 1580 in order to supply the "Spanish Riding Stables" in Vienna. The farm was transferred to Piber (Styria) when Lipizza found itself no longer part of Austria. The "High School" with its particular gaits, turns and figures and its impressive trained jumps (the Prince Eugen monument on the Heldenplatz, by the way, shows a horse rearing up in the "Levade"), is today only practised in its centuries old traditional form at the Spanish Riding School. Reserved exclusively to the court public until 1918, and saved at the end of the Second World War with the help of the American general and Lipizzaner fan Paton with the assistance of tanks (the spectacular *Flight of the White Stallions* was filmed by Walt Disney in 1953), the Spanish Riding School is today one of the top attractions of Vienna.

The animals can be seen in their venerable boxes during a visit to the Lipizzaner Museum, at their morning exercises, or bringing the city traffic to a standstill as they cross the road between the Stallburg and the Imperial Palace on their way down the Reitschulgasse as they are taken from the Stallburg to the Winter Riding School for their morning exercises every Tuesday to Saturday at 10.00. With a little luck, tickets can be obtained for the regular performances in the incomparably beautiful Winter Riding School. The sight of these magnificent animals prancing beneath the sparkling crystal chandeliers according to a centuries-old ritual brings the magic of the Baroque back to life. It was in the magnificent "swan-white" room with its gallery supported by forty-six columns, built by J.E. Fischer von Erlach from 1729–1735, that the famous Carousels used to take place, splendid riding festivals in which the Court took part. The "Lipizzaner Temple", as the Viennese called it, was also the venue for other major events. Thus it was here that Beethoven conducted a "monster concert" with one thousand musicians during the Congress of Vienna, and, in the year of revolution 1848, it was here that the first meeting of the Imperial Council took place. Today, the room is reserved for the performances of the High School of Riding.

Performance by the Spanish Riding School in the White Hall of the Winter Riding School.

Augustinerkirche (Church of the Augustinian Friars). From 1634–1783 the church, also reachable from Josefsplatz, was the imperial parish church where the weddings of the Imperial Family took place. It was here that Archduchess Marie-

Louise married Napoleon in 1810, with Archduke Karl acting as proxy, and in the same way her sister Leopoldine married Dom Pedro, later to become Emperor of Brazil. And it was in this church in 1854 that Emperor Franz Joseph married Elisabeth of Bavaria in a magnificent setting. Fifteen thousand candles shone, one thousand invited guests were present. The Archbishop of Vienna and over seventy bishops and prelates celebrated the marriage of the couple, whose close kinship had made a papal dispensation necessary. The whole of Vienna was on the streets to celebrate the wedding which, however, like many of the weddings concluded in this church, was to enjoy but little good fortune.

Schönbrunn Palace. After her wedding, Empress Elisabeth spent a large part of her early married years in Schönbrunn Palace, whose long and turbulent history makes it the most important cultural monument in Austria. It was in the east wing of the palace that Franz Joseph I was born in 1830. It was here that he spent the summer months of his childhood. Later, Schönbrunn was to become his favourite residence, where he spent most of his long life and where he died in 1916. When he ascended the throne in 1848, he moved into the west wing. His **Apartment**, to which the *Blue Staircase* led, consisted of the *audience room* (known as the *Nut-Wood Room*, with its valuable wood panelling from the time of Maria Theresia, and the *work room* and *bedroom* whose furnishing reflected the monarch's somewhat Spartan style. The "English toilet" in the doorway was only installed in 1899 – no provisions had been made for sanitary facilities in the palace. Since the Kaiser had a distaste for modern technology, he had the telephone installed not in his workroom but in this toilet.

The Equestrian Room with the so-called Marshal's Table.

The **Elisabeth Apartment**, also in the west wing, centres on a representative *salon* in the neo-rococo style, which served for the reception of personal visitors. It is connected to the joint *bedroom*, the *toilet room* and the *writing room*, the most private area and linked to Franz Joseph's apartment via the *terrace cabinet*. The salon also adjoins the rooms for family gatherings: the *dining room*, the *Cercle room* and the *consultation room* for representative purposes (later, it was here that the youngest daughter Marie Valerie lived). The ground floor rooms beneath this apartment were used by Elisabeth as an intimate **Garden Apartment** from 1863 on, together with a large salon and the usual gymnastics room, a fireplace made of Carraro marble and upholstery in Elisabeth's favourite colour, lilac. A terrace led to the Imperial Family's chamber garden. Elisabeth's children also lived on the ground floor, Gisela on the garden side and Crown Prince Rudolf in the **Crown Prince Apartments** from 1867 on. After her marriage to Archduke Franz Salvator, in 1890, Marie Valerie moved into the part known as the *Valerie Wing*.
It was in Schönbrunn that Elisabeth's life as the future Empress of Austria began. It was here that she spent the first night after her arrival in Vienna in 1854. And it was here that the ceremonial entry into the Imperial City began the next day. From 1860 on, she spent more and more time in

The Great Gallery in Schönbrunn Palace.

Schönbrunn. She could pursue her beloved riding in the palace park and in the Winter Riding School (today the Imperial Carriage Museum). Later she went for long walks in the palace gardens.
After Elisabeth's death, Franz Joseph lived in Schönbrunn for another eighteen years. The unoccupied rooms of the palace were opened to the public during the later years of his life (the gardens had been open to the public as an area of recreation since Maria Theresia's times). The splendid *Great Gallery* was used by the court as the stately venue for festivals and banquets. Franz Joseph preferred the adjoining *Small Gallery* for official occasions; in his old age he used the Great Gallery for walks in winter instead of the garden, and the hall was heated specially for this purpose. The large gallery was electrified in 1900 with 1,104 light bulbs. Thomas Alva Edison, the inventor of the incandescent light bulb, personally came to Vienna in order to supervise the installation of the electrical equipment in the palace. Today, Schönbrunn Palace and Park are amongst the most popular destinations for international culture tourists and were put on the list of the UNESCO's World Cultural Heritage in 1997.
Wagenburg (Imperial Carriage Museum). The former Winter Riding School contains over sixty historic state carriages, sleighs and sedan chairs together with imperial shabracks and liveries from the period 1690 to 1918. The showpiece of the collection is the four-ton highly decorated Imperial Coach which, drawn by eight white horses, was used from 1745 onwards for weddings and coronations. The black-varnished funeral coach drawn by eight black horses carried the Habsburgs on

their final journey to the Imperial Vault. The display also includes Emperor Franz Joseph's state carriage and the coach that took "Sisi" to Geneva – from which she did not return alive. The Railway Museum, a part of the Technical Museum, contains the splendid Court Salon Carriage (built in 1873) from the Empress's special train that carried her incessantly but luxuriously through Europe.

The Hietzing Urban Railway Court Pavilion. When Otto Wagner built the Vienna Urban Railway from 1894–1898, an elegant stop was also built at Schönbrunn and reserved for use by the Imperial Family, which at most happened twice. The Jugendstil waiting room is the only building by Wagner where the interior has remained practically complete, and as such represents a unique exhibition object; today it is an annex of the Historical Museum.

Hermes Villa. One of the most attractive – and nearest – destinations in the Vienna Woods is the *Lainz Animal Reserve*. And here, not far from the Lainz Gate, stands the Hermes Villa, a hunting castle in the historicist style, commissioned by Emperor Franz Joseph for his restless wife and built by the Ringstrasse architect Carl von Hasenauer from 1882–1886. No doubt he hoped that this would tie her more to Vienna. Here, Elisabeth could be close to him and yet far from the Imperial ceremonies. But the hope was in vain. Elisabeth never felt at home here. The Villa derives its name from the statue of Hermes in front of the building (Elisabeth's favourite god in Greek mythology was Hermes, the god of travel). The rooms, including the gymnasium in the style of Pompeii, were decorated by the painters Gustav Klimt and Hans Makart, and others. The opulent furnishings of the bedroom, also known as the " Makart Salon", includes frescos containing motifs from Elisabeth's favourite Shakespearean play, *A Midsummer Night's Dream*, and have survived intact.
Today the Palace is the venue for special exhibitions of the Historical Museum of the City of Vienna. It also contains a restaurant, and in summer it is in the Villa's stables that the Lipizzaner spend their holidays.

Laxenburg Palace. This old hunting residence passed into the Habsburgs' possession in 1306. They rebuilt the palace and added pleasure gardens and an animal reserve. The large park, always the particular attraction of this imperial country residence, was frequently redesigned to suit the taste of the time. Emperor Franz, for whom Laxenburg was the favourite abode, added an extra attraction in the form of the large pond and the Franzensburg (a neo-gothic "memorial palace" without any residential function). The imperial family's residence had been the Blue Court since approximately 1760. It was here that Elisabeth and Franz Joseph spent their honeymoon and also some of the first years of their marriage. It was here that their second daughter, Gisela was born in 1856, and was ceremoniously baptised in the large dining room – as was Rudolf two years later. In 1859, during the Lombardy War, Elisabeth set up a military hospital for the wounded in one of the Court buildings (the "*Grünne Haus*"). At the time of Emperor Franz Joseph, the roughly thirty-five buildings of various kinds were subject to imperial and royal administration. Their current uses are also very varied, including commercial operations, offices, apartments, scientific and museum facilities. The greatest attraction is the park, where you can walk, visit the castle, lie on the grass or boat on the pond – or go skating in winter. On the edge of the park there is a leisure centre with swimming pool, campsite and crazy golf.

Mayerling Palace. This former hunting palace of Crown Prince Rudolf is a somewhat gloomy memorial, and is roughly 40 km south west of Vienna, not far from the Heiligenkreuz Monastery (can be reached by bus from the Wien Mitte bus terminal). Even today, no one knows exactly what happened here. The facts: on the evening of January 30th, 1889, two bodies were discovered in the bedroom – the thirty-one year old Crown Prince Rudolf, the only son of Elisabeth and Franz Joseph, and his seventeen-year-old mistress Mary Freiin von Vetsera. Both had been shot. Was it really murder and/or suicide? The court did its best to hush-up the scandal, thus encouraging rumours. At the end of the 1980s, a businessman stole Mary Vetsera's bones from the vault at the Heiligenkreuz cemetery, thus bringing a new flood of visitors to Mayerling. In fact, there is very little to be seen of the original scene. Franz Joseph rapidly had a Carmelite monastery and church built at the scene of the tragedy. Memorial rooms in the convent contain furniture, paintings and illustrations – such as Rudolf on his death-bed, mourned by his family. Of course, Franz Joseph thought little of his son's liberal political opinions and of his way of life. Elisabeth, too, had had little time for him but after his death fell into deep mourning.

Imperial Burial Vault. In 1848, the traveller Theresa Bacheracht described "a wonderful ceremony at the funeral of the Imperial Majesties in Vienna." The Senior Seneschal had to knock three times at the door to the Kapuzinerkirche (Church of the Capuchin Monks), and each time the doorkeeper asked: "Who is there?" Twice the deceased titles are listed, and twice the coffin is refused entrance. It is only after the Seneschal humbled himself by saying "And so I ask for entry for the sinner", that the door was opened.

Since time immemorial the Habsburgs had been laid to rest in their venerable vaults according to this ritual. 145 members of the royal family, including 12 emperors and 16 empresses, are buried in the Imperial Vaults, the only outsider being Countess Fuchs, Maria Theresia's governess. The last to arrive was Empress Zita (1989). The Franz Joseph Vault contains Emperor Franz Joseph between the more luxuriant tombs of his wife Elisabeth and Crown Prince Rudolf, of whom his morally strict father said that he had died like a tailor. The centre of the complex, the Maria Theresia Vault, contains the sumptuous double tomb of Maria Theresia and her husband Franz Stephan von Lothringen, a masterpiece of rococo sculpture designed in 1753 by Balthasar Ferdinand Moll. Next to it, in stark contrast, is the simple coffin of Joseph II.

The Capuchin Monks had been called to Vienna as early as 1617 by Empress Anna during the Counter-reformation in order to found a monastery on the Neuer Markt that was also to be her burial place and that of her husband Emperor Matthias. The foundation stone was laid in 1622 by Emperor Ferdinand II, and the bodies of the imperial couple Matthias and Anna were buried there in 1633. Their simple "Founder's Vault" was the start of what was later to become the sumptuous burial vault of the Habsburgs – without doubt one of the most curious monuments in the history of Austria and in *pietas Austriae.*

The hearts of the Habsburgs were interred in the "Herzgrüftl" in the Augustinian Church, while their bodies were buried in the Imperial Burial Vault in the Capuchin Church.

The Ringstrasse Tour

In 1857, in a hand-written order, Emperor Franz Joseph ordered the razing of the old, now superfluous fortifications in order to create space for a long-planned expansion of the city. The demolition work was begun in 1858. The only remains of the old wall that survived the destruction are the Mölker Bastion (opposite the University) the Augustinerkirche Bastion near the Albertina, the Coburg Bastion (near the Parkring) and the Dominikaner Bastion (near the Stubenring). On the site thus made free, the new boulevard of Vienna was constructed, a ring road around the inner city lined by major public buildings. The construction was financed by selling the remaining land to aristocrats, industrialists and rich citizens.
On May 1st, 1865, the Emperor opened the boulevard, 4 km long and 57 metres wide, and capable of being driven on, although the buildings which were later to create the "Ringstrasse style" were still missing. The hereditary and moneyed aristocracy came together to create the "Ringstrasse Company", which not only constructed most of the buildings but also erected a number of sumptuous palaces for themselves along the Ring. The "old days" were gone for good. The citadel was becoming a city, and the period of promoterism was beginning.
Few cities have changed their appearance to such an extent in such a short time. Fifteen major public buildings were constructed between 1860 and 1890 along the Ringstrasse and its two rows of trees, all in architectural styles from the past, turning Vienna into a museum of historical architecture. The only religious building is the Votivkirche (Votive Church), and it had been commenced earlier. By the 1880s, the present appearance of the Ringstrasse was essentially complete – an unprecedented historicist work of art. It is true that the actual artistic value of the individual buildings, on which the most prominent architects of the time worked, remained disputed, but the outstanding architectural achievement is acknowledged even today.

The buildings on the Ringstrasse

The Ringstrasse does not, in fact, make a complete ring, since once side is formed by the Franz-Josephs-Kai along the Danube Canal. Our tour begins at the Urania and ends at the Rossau Barracks. Nevertheless it is possible to go around the Ring by tram, observing the row of monumental buildings on one of the most attractive sightseeing routes in Europe.
Urania (Urania Strasse 1). Built in 1909 according to plans by the Jugendstil architect Max Fabiani, the Urania with its planetarium, cinema and lecture halls continues to carry out its original function as a centre for public education.
Government Buildings (Stubenring 1) This mighty neo-Baroque complex was constructed between 1909 and 1913 as the Imperial War Ministry, and today houses a number of ministries. The original purpose of the building is reflected in the allegorical relief representations of battle and victory and the bronze 16 metre span two-headed eagle on the roof, as well as in the equestrian *statue of Field Marshall Radetzky*, a hero of the war against Italy, in front of the main gate.
Postsparkasse (Post Office Savings Bank) (Georg-Coch-Platz 2). Set somewhat back from the road, this building represents a milestone in the history of modern architecture. The Jugendstil work was designed by Otto Wagner, and was built between 1904 and 1912. Its main hall is well worth visiting.
Academy of Applied Art (Stubenring 5). Built between 1875 and 1877 by Heinrich von Ferstel as an extension to his **Museum** (today the MAK) in the style of the Italian Renaissance. The facade of the brick building was decorated in colour, including

sgraffito paintings and Majolica medallions showing portraits of various famous artists.
Karl Lueger Monument (Dr.-Karl-Lueger-Platz). Unveiled in 1926, this monument commemorates the Christian-Social mayor and father of the period of promoterism in Vienna.
City Park (Parkring). Opened in 1862, this large park extends along both banks of the River Wien, to which some steps lead. Worth seeing are the *Jugendstil portal* through which the river, built over by houses and roads in many places, once again comes out into the open, as well as the pavilions, walls, stairways, and riverbank promenades. The terrace of the Café Meierei Stadtpark (April – October, daily 9.00–21.00) near the Hilton Hotel offers an attractive view. On the Ringstrasse side of the park there is a *spa salon* (1867) whose terrace in summer is full of tourists listening to the Waltz Concerts over coffee and cakes. Appropriately, the splendid *monument to Johann Strauss the Younger*, is close by – a marble and gilded bronze work and a very popular motif for tourist cameras. There are also numerous other monuments in the park, such as those to Hans Makart, Anton Bruckner and Franz Schubert.
Hotel Imperial (Kärntner Ring 16). Vienna's most imposing hotel, the lodging place for state visitors to the Republic of Austria, was constructed 1862–1865 as a palace for the Duke of Württemberg. It is here that the Kärntner Ring begins, where once "high society" used to take its strolls. Even today, this once elegant avenue contains some of the most luxurious hotels in Vienna. Next to the Imperial stands the Bristol and the Grand Hotel (today the ANA Grand Hotel) re-opened in 1994 and extended by the elegant "Ringstrasse Galleries" Shopping Mall by the architect Wilhelm Holzbauer.

The Post Office Savings Bank Building built by Otto Wagner, 1904–12.

Musikvereinssaal (Hall of the Music Association) (Bösendorferstrasse 12). A block away from the Kärntner Ring stands this reddish building constructed between 1867 and 1869 in a style reminiscent of antiquity, by Theophil Hansen for the Gesellschaft für Musikfreunde (Society of the Friends of Music). It is world-famous for its *Golden Hall* with its unique acoustics, the venue of the annual New Year's Concert by the Vienna Philharmonic Orchestra.

The foyer of the State Opera House.

Staatsoper (State Opera House) (Opernring 2). The Opera House (at the time the Imperial and Royal Court Opera House) was in 1869 the first monumental construction to be completed on the new Ringstrasse. It was almost completely burnt down during the Second World War, and was reopened in 1955 with a performance of Beethoven's *Fidelio*. Today, it is regarded as one of the best opera houses in the world.

Akademie der Bildenden Künste (Academy of Fine Arts) (Schillerplatz 3). This building is set back from the road a little and was built and richly decorated in the style of the Italian Renaissance by Theophil Hansen. This Danish architect was one of the busiest architects of the Ringstrasse and was, himself, a teacher at the Academy. His most famous successor as teacher of architecture was Otto Wagner. Inside the building, the main hall is well worth seeing with its collection of plaster casts and impressive ceiling paintings by Anselm Feuerbach. The Academy is world famous, particularly for its *picture gallery*.

Burggarten (Palace Garden) (Opernring/Burgring). This attractive park, known until 1919 as the Imperial Garden, was created in the English style in 1823, and was exclusively reserved to the members of the imperial family. It contains a pond, expansive lawns which the young people of Vienna bitterly fought to use in the 1970s, an impressive *palm house* that also contains a café in summer, as well as the *monuments* of Franz I, Franz Joseph I and Wolfgang Amadeus Mozart.

Äusseres Burgtor (Outer Palace Gate) (Burgring). This gate is the entrance to the Imperial Castle from the Burgring and was constructed after Napoleon had demolished the Palace Bastion in 1809. This had left the Palace unprotected and it was decided in 1821/24 to place this mighty gate at the end of the newly created Heldenplatz to commemorate the battle of Leipzig – against Napoleon. In 1934, it was converted into a memorial for the dead of the First World War, and was added to in 1945 by a monument to the members of the Austrian resistance against fascism. The bronze crucifix next to the palace gate (on the side facing the palace) commemorates a visit by Pope John Paul II in 1983.

Neue Burg (New Palace) (Burgring/Heldenplatz).According to the plan by Gottfried Semper, this was to be part of a monumental "imperial forum" similar to the Louvre, which would also include the two planned Imperial Museums on the other side of the Ringstrasse. However, the ambitious project was never executed. The Neue Burg (1881–1913) was constructed according to Carl Hasenauer's plans in the neo-renaissance monumental style. Today the Ringstrasse wing of the New Palace contains the *"Ethnological Museum"*. In the "Wing of Columns", there is a reading room and a catalogue room of the Austrian National Library, as well as three museums (the *Ephesos Museum*, the *Weapons Collection* and the *Collection of Old Musical Instruments*); it was from the terrace above the central entrance that Hitler announced Austria's Anschluss to Nazi Germany in March 1938. The left wing (Festival Hall Wing) serves as a congress centre.

Kunsthistorisches Museum (Museum of Fine Arts) / **Naturhistorisches Museum** (Natural History Museum) (Burgring 5 and 7). The two former Imperial Museums were constructed from 1872–81 as mirror images of each other in the style of the Italian Renaissance (although the Museum of Fine Arts was only opened in 1891). The square between them is dominated by the **Maria Theresia Memorial**, one of the most monumental statues in Vienna. Its pedestal was created by Carl Hasenauer, the statue by the sculptor Caspar Zumbusch. Unveiled in 1887 after thirteen years of work, the memorial shows the Empress on a huge pedestal, sitting on her throne, surrounded by her generals (on horseback) and her advisers (on foot); even her composers are immortalised – Gluck, Haydn and the child prodigy, Mozart, can be seen in the archways of the high relief.
Republiksdenkmal (Monument to the Republic) (Dr.-Karl-Renner-Ring). Erected in 1928 on the tenth anniversary of the founding of the Republic, this monument stands before the former Epstein Palace and shows three politicians who played a decisive role in the establishment and the maintenance of the First Republic: Victor Adler (the great unifying force amongst the Austro-Marxists), Jakob Reumann (the first Social Democratic mayor of Vienna) and Ferdinand Hainusch (who influenced the Republic's social policies). The monument was removed by the Austro-fascists in 1934 and returned to its position on November 12th, 1948. It is also a reminder of the fact that the Ringstrasse is not only an elegant boulevard and an imposing background against which imperial and civic power was developed, but also a political meeting place for the population. Even today, all kinds of demonstrations, parades, processions and the traditional May parades use the wide Ringstrasse, usually from the Opera House to the Town Hall.
Parliament (Dr.-Karl-Renner-Ring 3).This building by Theophil von Hansen is in the

Hall of dinosaurs in the Natural History Museum.

style of ancient Greece – Greece being regarded as the mother of democracy – and its sophisticated clarity makes it the most attractive of all the buildings on the Ring. Today, the National Council and the Federal Council meet in the two-storey building behind the elegantly curved ramps. It was on this ramp that the Republic was promulgated in 1918, a Republic that took over the building unchanged. The pediment above the main entrance still shows allegories of the 17 crown countries of the monarchy. The *Pallas Athene fountain* in front of the building represents an allegory of the most important rivers of the monarchy in the form of recumbent figures –

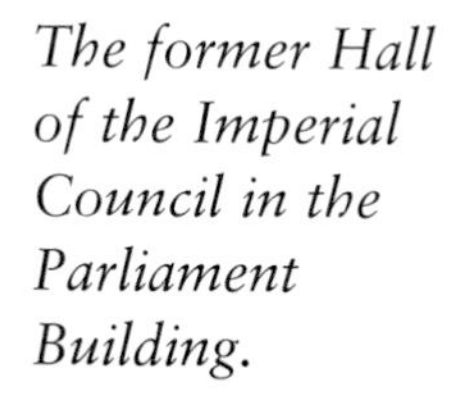

The former Hall of the Imperial Council in the Parliament Building.

The Theseus Temple in the Volksgarten.

the Danube and the Inn (at the front), the Elbe and the Moldau (at the back). Above them, two female figures represent the legislature and the executive, towered over by the Goddess herself, enthroned on the column.

Volksgarten (People's Gardens) (Dr.-Karl-Renner-Ring). Laid out in 1821–23 after the Palace Bastions were destroyed by Napoleon, the Volksgarten – unlike the "Imperial Gardens" (Burggarten) created at the same time – was dedicated to the general public. For this reason, it was laid out with strict symmetry, expressly in order to be able to supervise the public – after all, this was in Metternich's police state. In the centre stands the *Theseus Temple*, a copy of the antique Theseion in Athens, built by Pietro Nobile from 1821–23. The northern corner contains the *monument to Empress Elisabeth*, flanked by cool marble benches.

Burgtheater (National Theatre) (Dr.-Karl-Renner-Ring 2). When the National Theatre was opened in 1888 as the last of the major buildings on the Ring, the critics were just as vicious as for the Opera House before it. The old National Theatre on the Michaelerplatz had been a very intimate affair, and it was now necessary to get used to the "Imperial Court Theatre" seating an audience of 1,300. Nevertheless, its designer Carl Hasenauer, had taken particular account of the city's conservative habits. The stage remained a picture-frame stage, simply further away from the public, the hierarchy of boxes and galleries was retained, the ceremonial stairways and foyers were richly ornamented with frescos (including some by Gustav Klimt) and busts, and thus it was indeed a sumptuous setting for a theatre that paid particular attention to tradition and class consciousness.

Neues Rathaus (New Town Hall) (Rathausplatz 1). The way to the Vienna Town Hall is through the *Rathauspark* with its fountains, ancient trees (some exotic)and countless monuments (including to Ferdinand Georg Waldmüller, Johann Strauss the Elder, Josef Lanner, the physicist Ernst Mach, the philosopher Josef Popper-Lynkeus, and the politicians Karl Seitz, Theodor Körner and Karl Renner). The building is based on Belgian Gothic and was designed by the Swabian Friedrich von Schmidt. Completed in 1883 in the same year as the Parliament building, the huge complex became a magnificent neo-gothic edifice of superlatives, with open arcades, loggias, balconies, lancet windows, courtyards and a wealth of sculpted ornamentation. The ceremonial hall is the largest in Austria. The monumental arcade courtyard is today an events venue (e.g. for concerts of the "musical summer"). The *Schmidthalle* at the rear contains the *City Information Office*. The *Volkshalle* is also open to the public, and is often used for exhibitions. At the top of the almost 100 metre high main tower stands the "Iron Man of the Town Hall", 6 metres high and weighing 1.8 tons with his standard, a landmark of Vienna. The large *Rathausplatz* is an extremely popular events venue where there is almost always something happening, from the ceremonial opening of the Vienna Festival or the popular summer Opera Film Festival to the Christkindl Market and the "Vienna Ice Dream", the most beautiful ice skating rink in Vienna.

New University (Dr.-Karl-Lueger-Ring 1). Since the *old University* had long become too small, Heinrich Ferstel constructed this massive new building in the strict style of the Italian Renaissance, the era that had been the start of the "Golden Age" of western science. Around the turn of the century Gustav Klimt produced three paintings for the main hall, but these caused such a scandal that finally the painter withdrew what he called his "faculty paintings" – allegories of philosophy, jurisprudence and medicine. The main painting is by his colleague Franz Matsch.
Votivkirche (Votive Church) (Rooseveltplatz). In February 1853, Emperor Franz Joseph survived an assassination attempt. This caused his brother Maximilian, later the Emperor of Mexico, to suggest the construction of a thanksgiving and penitential church. The foundation stone of this neogothic votive church was laid in 1856, and after twenty-three years work, the church was consecrated in 1879 on the occasion of the imperial couple's silver wedding anniversary, when the whole of Vienna came out to marvel at Hans Makart's gigantic parade. The architect was Heinrich Ferstel, and the costs of the two 99 metre high towers were borne by the City of Vienna. The church, in part an imitation of Cologne Cathedral, contains an *organ* with over 3,700 pipes, the *Antwerp Altar* – a masterpiece of Flemish carving from the 15th century – and the over 400-year-old *tomb of Count Niklas Salm*, the defender of Vienna during the first Turkish siege in 1529, as well as a colossal painting by Gustave Doré (1832–83), *Christ leaving the Pretorium.*
Börse (Stock Exchange) (Schottenring 16). In 1877, the Vienna Stock Exchange, which had been located at a number of different addresses since it was founded in 1771 (last of all in what is today the Palais Ferstel in the Herrengasse), moved into the new neo-renaissance building by Theophil Hansen.

In winter Vienna's most attractive skating rink is to be found in front of the Town Hall; in the background, the National Theatre.

Rossau Barracks (Schlickplatz). The army's reservations about the demolition of the fortifications in 1858 were overcome by the construction of two barracks; the Franz Joseph Barracks (later demolished; today the Post Office Savings Bank occupies the spot) and the Rossau Barracks on the other side of the Schottenring. The red-brick building in the style of a medieval castle was constructed from 1865-1869, in order to provide the army with a presence in the city. It later served as a police barracks and today is used as a police station.

JUGENDSTIL IN VIENNA

In April 1897, the *Secession* Artists Association was founded in Vienna, a unique variety of the European Jugendstil or Art Nouveau movement. It was started when the tempestuous "youths" resigned from the established *Künstlerhaus* and set up the "Association of Austrian Fine Artists, Secession" with its leading figures Otto Wagner and Gustav Klimt. The aim of the movement's programme was for art to penetrate all aspects of life. The Secessionists wanted to build and furnish the homes of the people. This may also have been true of the historicism of the Ringstrasse era, in particular the opulent Hans Makart. But the new solution was to abandon imi-

tation gold and unnecessary luxury, replacing them with authenticity of materials, utilitarianism and intelligent forms. Its theoretical journal was the *Ver Sacrum*, which was to become an icon of the Vienna Jugendstil thanks to its design and its famous authors. The measure of the modern way of life was set by the *Wiener Werkstätte* (Vienna Workshops) founded in 1903 by Josef Hoffmann and Koloman Moser, creating a range of products from useful table cutlery to the design of fashionable villas. Today, these are highly in demand and achieve enormous prices at auctions.

But even at the time, this new movement, despite all the controversy, did not encounter a wholly hostile reception, as many of its member felt, but was indeed well supported by parts of the public sector. For instance Otto Wagner's buildings made a significant architectural mark on the development of city on the Danube's into a major European metropolis, and he himself was a teacher at the Academy of Fine Arts. Josef Hoffmann taught at the School of Industrial Arts, and Koloman Moser designed new stamps for the Post Office. The secessionist Alfred Roller was chief stage designer at the Imperial Opera House under Gustav Mahler. Finally, the opening of the first exhibition of the avantgarde was honoured by the personal appearance of Emperor Franz Joseph himself, invited by the famous Viennese painter Rudolf von Alt. The latter had joined the movement at the age of eighty five, and when the Emperor expressed his surprise, replied: "I might be really old, your Majesty, but I still feel young enough to start again."

The most attractive Jugendstil works

Secession (1st District). One of the most important Jugendstil works in Vienna, this exhibition building of the Secessionists was constructed on the edge of the Karlsplatz in 1897–98 by Joseph Maria Olbrich, one of Otto Wagner's most important pupils. The building is crowned by a striking lace-like dome made of gilded laurel leaves, known popularly as the "cabbage head". Over the entrance stands the prominent motto of the Vienna Secessionists: "To each time its Art, to Art its freedom". The bronze statue of *Mark Anthony* to

Figure on the roof of Otto Wagner's Post Office Savings Bank.

The Otto Wagner houses at Linke Wienzeile 38 and 40, two icons of Jugenstil.

the right of the pavilion is by the sculptor Arthur Strasser (1900). The very first exhibitions created a sensation. They showed "specific modern art", but at the same time opened up Vienna to the movements of European art. The *Secession* Artists Association still exists, and its building is still an exhibition and events venue.

The **Beethoven Frieze** is once again on display in the Secession. As a means of underlining the importance of Max Klinger's Beethoven Monument (today in the Gewandhaus in Leipzig), the artists of the Secession decided to make their Association's fourteenth exhibition a total work of art, with Gustav Klimt to design an entire room. The result was an extraordinary representation of the content of Beethoven's *9th Symphony*. However, the critics and the population at large showed little understanding of his large-area ornaments and naturalistic nudes. The general opinion was "appalling". After the exhibition ended, the Frieze was removed and put into storage. The restored work has been on display again in the basement of the building since 1986. Klimt's Beethoven Frieze (total length 26 m) is one of the most significant works of the Jugendstil.

The painter Gustav Klimt (1862–1918), without doubt the most famous artist of the Viennese Jugendstil, was the President of the Secession in its early years. He designed the title pages for its journal *Ver Sacrum*, as well as posters. He resigned in 1905, founding the *Klimt Group*, whose comprehensive *Vienna 1908 Art Exhibition* was the most impressive presentation of modern art. Some of Klimt's works can be seen at the following places: the Austrian Gallery of the 19th and 20th century, Upper Belvedere (paintings); the Museum of Modern Art Ludwig Foundation Vienna (paintings); the Albertina Collection of Graphic Art (drawings); the Museum of Fine Arts (stairway); the National Theatre (stairways).

Otto Wagner Ensemble on Wienzeile (6th District, Linke Wienzeile 38 and 40, and Köstlergasse 3). Not far from the Secession, only a few hundred metres towards the edge of the city, stands a magnificent Jugendstil ensemble of three houses by Otto Wagner. It was with this design that Vienna's great modern architect finally broke with the styles on the Ringstrasse and took up cudgels on behalf of the principles of the Secession, according to which the function of a building should determine its form. As a result, the different purposes – shops, offices and apartments – were no longer hidden behind a uniform front, but were emphasised by very different areas of the facade. At Linke Wienzeile 38, the architect exploited the corner position and applied a two-part rounding of the facade, placing an airy loggia on the top storey and above it sculptures by Othmar Schimkowitz. The gold decoration on the facade is by Koloman Moser. **House No. 40**, the famous "Majolica House" with its practically indestructible facade, once again shows Otto Wagner's preference for unusual materials: iron for the columns and the parapet, colourful ceramic tiles with delightful floral patterns for the facade. The houses were completed in 1898/99. Wagner was also responsible for the nearby Kettenbrückengasse underground station (former urban railway station).
Urban Railway Pavilions. In 1898, the first steam-operated line of the new urban railway was opened in the presence of the Emperor. The railway system was built according to the artistic and technical plans of Otto Wagner, and formed a curve around the inner city. The outer regions were served by direct trains. The transport network was further extended by the "suburban line" (also by Otto Wagner) linking the city's outer districts, and still in operation today, but the architect's visionary proposal for the construction of an underground railway remained unheeded. For the 40 km long urban railway network, Wagner constructed 36 station buildings, including Jugendstil jewels such as the "Karlsplatz" (two pavilions) and "Stadtpark" stations, the "Hietzing court pavilion" as well as all the bridges, galleries etc. According to Josef Hoffmann, the railway was "the only one of its kind that did not disfigure the town but created a series of the most attractive urban images ...", and is today part of the underground railway network.
Postsparkasse (Post Office Savings Bank) (1st District, Georg-Coch-Platz 2). In 1903, Otto Wagner won the competition for the construction of the Imperial and Royal Austrian Post Office Savings Bank. The building was completed in 1912, a showpiece of modern architecture, artistically revolutionary, functional and worked out to the smallest detail. It was the first modern building on the Ringstrasse and boasts a facade of thin marble slabs fixed with bolts. To decorate the building, Wagner used the newly fashionable material aluminium, also applying this material to the outlets of the hot air heating, which created a particular sensation at the time (today no longer in operation). The office rooms were fitted with sliding walls to allow them to be easily adjusted to requirements. Functionality and aesthetics are also combined in the monumental *Kassensaal* (Main Hall), where even the radiators are works of art. Modern materials, glass and steel, predominate. The building and its facilities, also by Wagner, were well received. "Amazing how well the people fit in", the old Emperor is said to have commented. And even today, the bank employees swear that it continues to meet the requirements of a modern banking institution.
Kirche St. Leopold am Steinhof (the Church of St. Leopold at the Steinhof psychiatric hospital) (14th District, Baumgartnerhöhe). The Steinhof, at the time one of the world's most modern psychiatric hospitals, was among the municipal achievements of the

Top of the dome of Otto Wagner's Church am Steinhof.

Viennese mayor Karl Lueger. Otto Wagner made a plan for the entire facility, but was only commissioned to build the church, his only religious building. His modern idea of a church was to replace the long hall with a central construction to allow every visitor a good view. The building had to take account of special requirements. It had separate entrances for the men's and women's departments, the rows of benches were easy to supervise, the inclined floor was easy to clean. For the facade, Wagner used the same slab structure as on the Post Office Savings Bank. The bright symmetrical interior, without any columns, and with glass windows designed by Koloman Moser, is topped by a huge dome. Its roof is made of copper plates which, like the four angels above the entrance, were originally gilded and must once have seemed like a lighthouse in the rays of the sun on this hill in the west of Vienna.

The first buildings by Otto Wagner (1841–1918) were in the Ringstrasse style, before he built his most famous Jugendstil buildings at an advanced age. His interest in city planning, new building techniques and functional solutions made him the showcase architect of the Viennese Modern, influencing as a teacher practically the whole of the following generation of architects. Other buildings by Otto Wagner worth seeing are: *Villa Wagner 1* (1886/88). Today owned by the painter Ernst Fuchs. 14th District, Hüttelbergstrasse 26; *Villa Wagner 2* (1912/13). 14th District, Hüttelbergstrasse 28; *Wagner's "City Palace"* (1890/92). 3rd District, Rennweg 1; the house next-door, No. 3, is also by Wagner; *Nussdorfer Wehr* (system of locks on the Danube Canal, (1894/98). 19th District, near Nussdorfer Platz; *Schützenhaus "Staustufe Kaiserbad"* (Riflemen's clubhouse at the Kaiserbad lock) (1906/07). Danube Canal, at the level of the Schottenring underground station. *"Der Anker" insurance company building* (1895). 1st District, corner of Graben 10/Spiegelgasse 2; two monuments commemorate the great architect: his *Monument* designed by Josef Hoffmann. 1st District, corner of Makartgasse/Getreidemarkt and the *Tomb*. Designed by Wagner in person for himself and his family. 13th District, Hietzing Cemetery, Maxingstrasse 15, Group 13, Tomb 131

Loos House (1st District, 26 Michaelerplatz 3). In 1911 the architect Adolf Loos (1870–1933) completed his famous building opposite the Michaelerkirche – its smooth unbroken facade a shock for the Viennese, for never had there been such an entirely unornamented house. "House without eyebrows" was the name they

Facade of the Loos Haus on Michaelerplatz.

gave to the scandalous building that has gone down in architectural history as a construction of trail-blazing importance. Loos was not a Secessionist but one of the dominant architects of the Viennese Modern. Rejecting the tendency of the Jugendstil artists toward ornamentation, he vehemently opposed false appearances and committed himself to a total absence of ornamentation in architecture. His principles were embodied in shops (Loos, himself always elegantly dressed, was the architect of men's outfitters, e. g. *Kniže* on the Graben), the *American Bar* (1908/09) near the Kärntnerstrasse, and in the (no longer surviving) interior of the *Cafe Museum* in the Operngasse (1899). In 1931, he designed glasses for the Lobmeyr company (Kärntnerstrasse 26), which are still being manufactured today.

Zacherl House (1st District, Brandstätte 6). Josef Plečnik, a pupil of Otto Wagner and one of the most important men in the development of modern architecture, created this building in 1903/05, one of the most famous Jugendstil houses in Vienna. Peter Altenberg was so taken by the spectacular construction that he exclaimed: "Only poets should be allowed to live here!"

The House "Zum Weissen Engel" (1st District, Bognergasse 9). Oskar Laske, also a pupil of Wagner's, created this modern building for his father's construction company.

The Portois & Fix House (3rd District, Ungargasse 59–61). While Otto Wagner was working on the Majolica house at Linke Wienzeile 40, his former pupil Max Fabiani was designing the home and offices of the Portois & Fix building company, again a tiled building of elegant simplicity. Fabiani also designed the House Artaria (1900–02) and the Urania.

The Anker Clock (1st District, Hoher Markt 10–12). The flying buttress above the Rotgasse bears the famous and very popular Anker Clock designed by the painter Franz Matsch (1911/17), a former companion of Gustav Klimt.

Strudelhof Stairs (9th District, Liechtensteinstrasse, corner of Strudlhofgasse). These picturesque stairs were designed by Theodor Jäger and opened in 1910. Heimito von Doderer's novel of the same name (1951) made it world famous.

The Krieau Trotting Racing Association (2nd District, Prater, Trabrennstrasse, Südportalstrasse). The racecourse was founded in the 19th century but was considerably expanded in 1910. This latter work was carried out by three of Otto Wagner's pupils, and his influence is visible in the design of the stands and the use of materials such as iron and concrete.

In 1903 the artists Josef Hoffmann and Koloman Moser founded the **Wiener Werkstätte** (Vienna Workshops), a pinnacle of applied arts unequalled this century, with a modern approach that is still of relevance. Its range of high quality utility goods included furniture, crockery, cutlery, jewellery, wallpaper, book covers, postcards and fashions. Individual items can be seen nowadays in auction houses such as the Dorotheum, in the Museum of Applied Arts, in the Lobmeyr Glass Museum, and in the Historical Museum of the City of Vienna. The Vienna Workshop employed artists such as Klimt, Schiele and Kokoschka, but closed in 1931.

Unadulterated Jugenstil: The Engel Pharmacy in Bognergasse in the 1st District.

Vienna for Music Lovers

In the footsteps of the great composers

Wolfgang Amadeus Mozart

In September 1762, the Mozart family moved to Vienna, where the six-year-old Wolfgang together with his sister Nannerl performed on the harpsichord, violin and organ in the houses of the aristocracy. These performances culminated in a reception in Schönbrunn, where the child prodigy played before the Empress Maria Theresia. This was followed by other concert tours that gained "Wolferl" a tremendous reputation amongst the European aristocracy as a virtuoso and composer. Mozart (1756–1791), born in Salzburg as the son of the composer Leopold Mozart and his wife Anna, achieved international fame at an early age. From 1769, he was the leader of the Archbishop's Orchestra in Salzburg, but fell out with the Archbishop and went to Vienna in 1781, marrying Constanze Weber in the following year. Mozart was extremely productive and earned a lot (the legend of the impoverished genius is an invention), but his extravagant way of life frequently brought him into financial difficulties. He died at the lowest point of his financial crisis of "hot miliary fever" (probably feverish articular rheumatism) just when he was on the threshold of his first important operatic

Otmar Lang, maker of violins for the Vienna Philharmonic Orchestra and the State Opera House, in his violin-making and repair studio.

success. *The Magic Flute* was to be performed 200 times in Vienna alone before 1798. Historians claim that it was not necessary for Mozart to be given an unworthy third-class burial at the St. Marx Cemetery, since only a small additional payment would have prevented him being buried in the unmarked multiple grave prescribed for this class of burial. Be that as it may, the grave was forgotten, and it was only around 1850 that an unknown person planted a willow tree at the approximate spot.

Selected Mozart addresses

13th District, Schönbrunn Palace. On October 13, 1762, the young Mozart gave his legendary concert in the presence of Empress Maria Theresia, most probably in the Great Gallery. In 1786, Mozart's opera *The Theatre Director* was performed in the Orangerie. This hothouse, the worlds longest of its kind, was renovated in 1994/95, and is today the venue of the Schönbrunn Palace Concerts, which in particular focus on the most famous works of Johann Strauss the Younger and Mozart.

1st District, Am Hof 13, Palais Collalto. It was in this Baroque aristocratic palace (next to the Church of the Nine Choirs of Angels) that the six-year-old Mozart first performed before the Viennese public shortly before his musical audience at the Imperial Court.

1st District, Singerstrasse 7, Deutschordenshaus, first courtyard. Mozart lived here in 1781 with the household of the Salzburg Prince-Archbishop Graf Collorado. His request for permission to leave the post of leader of the orchestra led to a scene with the head kitchener Graf Arco, who was responsible for the music. It ended with Mozart being literally kicked out, and his employment was finished.

1st District, Domgasse 5, Figaro House. Mozart lived in this elegant apartment from 1784 to 1787 (today it is *the* Mozart memorial in Vienna). It was here that he composed his opera *The Marriage of Figaro*, and the only Goethe song he composed, *Das Veilchen.* This was not this house's only role in the history of Viennese music. In 1785, Joseph Haydn visited Mozart, followed in 1787 by the 16-year-old Beethoven. The highly talented 7-year-old Johann Nepomuk Hummel was accepted by Mozart as a pupil and lodged with him here for two years. Later, in 1862, Johannes Brahms visited the pianist Julius Epstein, who lived in this house.

Wolfgang Amadeus Mozart, painting by Joseph Lange, (incomplete, 1789).

1st District, Himmelpfortgasse 6. Since there was no dedicated concert hall in Vienna at the time, the role was often filled by tavern rooms. This was the case for the Jahn'sche Saal on the first storey of the Jahn restaurant (above today's Café Frauenhuber), which is associated with the works of major composers such as Beethoven and Mozart. Both also performed at Jahn's *morning concerts* in the Augarten. It was in the Jahn'sche Saal that Mozart gave his last performance in 1791.

1st District, Rauhensteingasse 8 = Kärntnerstrasse 19, where Mozart died. In the last year of his life, Mozart lived in the former "Small Imperial House". It was here that he wrote the *Requiem*, whose origins are wreathed in legend – a work commissioned through an anonymous messenger by someone who intended to pass the work off as his own composition. The "Steffl" department store stands on the site today, and on the 5th floor there is a Mozart memorial room displaying objects from the house of Mozart's death.
1st District, St. Stephen's Cathedral. On the outer wall on the north side of the cathedral, near the exit from the catacombs, there is a memorial plaque bearing the inscription: "It was here that the mortal remains of the immortal W. A. Mozart were blessed on December 6, 1791". It was also in St. Stephen's Cathedral that Mozart married Constanze.
3rd District, St. Marx Cemetery (3rd District, Leberstrasse 6–8). The romantic Mozart tombstone (No. 179) was erected in 1870 and marks the approximate spot of his burial place.
11th District, Central Cemetery, Group 32a, Grave No. 55. Mozart's grave of honour is nothing but a memorial, since his bones rest in St. Marx. The monument by Hans Gasser was unveiled at the St. Marx Cemetery, and later moved here.

"Mozart Grave" (the exact spot is unknown) at the St. Marx Cemetery.

1st District, Burggarten, Mozart Memorial. This memorial by Viktor Tilgner stood on the square in front of the Albertina from 1896 to 1945, and was erected in the Burggarten in 1953.
6th District, Linke Wienzeile/Millöckergasse, Theater an der Wien. The theatre director Emanuel Schickaneder, who had given the first performance of *The Magic Flute* in his Freihaus-Theater in 1791 (the libretto was also by him), opened the Theater an der Wien in 1801. Part of the building was torn down in 1902. The side entrance is the famous "Papageno Door". Above the classicist doorway, the actor can be seen in his favourite role – as Papageno. Schickaneder was Mozart's fellow freemason.
1st District, Fleischmarkt 11, Griechenbeisl. In this historic tavern's autograph room, prominent guests have for centuries left their permanent mark on the walls, and Mozart was no exception.

Ludwig van Beethoven

Beethoven (1770–1827) was the son of a family of musicians from Bonn, and at the early age of 14 became a member of the Court Orchestra of the Cologne Elector. He came to Vienna on a stipendium in 1792, to study under Joseph Haydn. He stayed, and it was here that he found his second home, where he was warmly welcomed by the music-loving Viennese aristocracy. He gave his first piano recital in 1795.
To begin with, Beethoven's works owed much to Mozart and Haydn. Around 1802, he began to break away from tradition and finally achieved an unprecedented independence. He is regarded as the pinnacle of Viennese classicism – and as the first musical "freelancer", who was no longer dependent on imperial commissions. Instead he was welcomed in the aristocratic salons. Prince Franz Josef Lobkowitz, in whose salon the *Eroica* was first heard, gave the composer a pension, Prince Andreas Rasumofsky made available his quartet, Prince Karl Lichnowsky his palace. Throughout all this, Beethoven stuck to his artistic independence and to his revolutionary and republican principles.
This restless composer often moved home, occasionally even outside Vienna, so that later Karl Kraus joked: "Vienna has some beautiful surroundings, to which Beethoven often fled." He preferred

to stay in what was then the village of Heiligenstadt, where he wrote his *"Heiligenstadt Testament"* in 1802. In this letter to his brother, Beethoven described the effects of the increasing deafness that was cutting him off more and more from society and his own works. In the end, the great composer could only communicate with the assistance of conversation books. At his death in 1827, a huge crowd of people paid him the last honours.

Selected Beethoven addresses

1st District, Mölkerbastei 8, Pasqualati House. Beethoven lived in this house several times between 1804 and 1815, and it is one of the most important Beethoven memorials in Vienna. Beethoven moved home 80 times in Vienna, and never lived anywhere longer than here, where a large number of his greatest works were created. Today the apartment is a museum.

19th District, Döblinger Hauptstrasse 92, Eroica House. Beethoven lived in the so-called Biederhof in 1807, mainly working on his *third symphony*, the Eroica. The Eroica House contains a memorial.

19th District, Probusgasse 6, the "Heiligenstadt Testament" Memorial. It was here on October 6, 1802, that Beethoven wrote the letter that he never sent to his brother and that has gone down in history as the *"Heiligenstadt Testament"*. In it he complains about the deafness that brought him on a health holiday to Heiligenstadt. The original is in Hamburg. The house contains an exhibition room of the Vienna Beethoven Society.

19th District, Beethoven Walk (by Kahlenbergerstrasse 69). The "Beethoven Walk" was Beethoven's favourite stroll, and the monument here was the first in Vienna. The metal bust by Ferdinand Fernkorn was unveiled in 1863.

6th District, Laimgrubengasse 22. Beethoven lived here near to his brother Johann in 1822/23. The house was built in 1782 and later converted, and contains a memorial by the Vienna Beethoven Society containing pictures and documents about Beethoven's stay here.

9th District, Schwarzspanierstrasse 15. At this address once stood the Schwarzspanierhof, which contained Beethoven's last Viennese apartment (1825–27). It was here that he lived, surrounded by friends and visitors, until his death. The modern building bears a memorial plaque to the composer, and to the right above the entrance, a bust of the composer. In 1903, the room in which he died was rented by the Jewish philosopher and Beethoven fan Otto Weininger, who then committed suicide in the room shortly afterwards.

Ludwig van Beethoven, painting by Ferdinand Georg Waldmüller (1823).

18th District, Währingerstrasse/Teschnergasse, Schubertpark. Unlike Mozart, Beethoven's burial was attended by a huge crowd. 20,000 people, including numerous celebrities, joined the funeral procession. On his grave was placed a simple pyramid-like gravestone with the inscription "Beethoven" – still there today. The cemetery was closed in 1873 and later transformed into the Schubertpark. However, Beethoven's and Schubert's graves can still be seen (the key to the commemorative grove is available free of charge at the nearby office on Mondays to Fridays, 7.00–15.00).

11th District, Central Cemetery, Group 32A, Grave No. 29. In 1888, Beethoven's bones were transferred here and buried in an honorary grave of the City of Vienna. The tombstone is an imitation of that in Währing.

1st District, Beethovenplatz, monument. In 1880, Caspar Zumbusch created the Beethoven monument donated by admirers of the composer, and one of the most important works by this great sculptor. An original cast model of this monument was put up in the foyer of the Vienna Concert House in 1927.

Franz Schubert

Franz Schubert (1797–1828), the epitome of the Viennese musical genius, composed a huge number of works during his short life. His roughly 1,000 compositions, a pinnacle of romantic music, include chamber music, masses, operas, Singspiele and symphonies. But above all, Schubert was responsible for a new musical form: the Lied, which, taking up old Viennese traditions, he raised to the level of an independent artistic form. The composer wrote roughly 600 songs, including *Die schöne Müllerin* and *Die Winterreise* cycles, for which posterity has given him the title of "Prince of songs".

Born the son of a school teacher, Schubert was a member of the Imperial Boy's Choir from 1808 to 1813; at that time the choir was conducted by Antonio Salieri, leader of the court orchestra and famous as Mozart's opponent at the Imperial Court. In 1814, he joined his father's school as an assistant, but left the parental home after three years, from then on leading an uncertain artist's existence continuously plagued by financial worries.

"Schubert Organ" in the Lichtental Parish Church.

With the exception of some brief instruction in composing by Salieri, Franz Schubert was self-taught. Ignored by the Imperial Court and without the support of aristocratic patrons, his life and his work developed against a middle class background and amongst a middle class circle of friends. With his modest existence and the melancholy that interrupted the conviviality that was later to be trivialised as cheerful "Schubertiades", Schubert was a typical figure of the Viennese Biedermeier. He did not achieve public success, and gave his last concert in March 1828. A few months later, at the age of 31, he died after a serious illness, only one year after his admired Beethoven. At his own request he was buried at the then Währing Local Cemetery next to the grave of Beethoven, whom he had never met during his lifetime. The tombstone, designed by his friend Franz von Schober, bears the commemorative words by the poet Franz Grillparzer: "Here music laid to rest a rich possession but even greater hopes."

Selected Schubert addresses

9th District, Nussdorferstrasse 54, Birthplace. It was in the kitchen of the "Zum roten Krebsen" suburban house that Schubert first saw the light of day in 1797, the 12th of 14 children. At the time, 17 families lived in this two-storey building, and 100 children were taught by Schubert's father on the ground floor. Today it is a museum with numerous items commemorating the composer, including his "trademark", the nickel spectacles that he wore while he slept so as to be able to write down the first notes of music as soon as he awoke.

9th District, Marktgasse 40, Schubertkirche (Schubert Church). It was in the Liechtental Parish Church of the 14 Auxiliary Saints that Schubert was baptised. As a boy he sang in the church choir, played the organ from 1812 to 1820 (the so called Schubert organ in the church is a reminder

The house in which Schubert was born in Nussdorfer Strasse; in the display cabinet, his reading spectacles.

of this time), and in 1814 conducted his *F major mass.* Therese Grob, Schubert's first unhappy love, was the soprano soloist.
1st District, Imperial Palace, Imperial Palace Chapel. Franz Schubert sang mass here as a choir boy from 1808 to 1812. When his voice broke, he wrote on a sheet of music: "Franz Schubert croaked for the last time on July 26, 812".
1st District, Spiegelgasse 9 "Göttweiger Hof". One of the few surviving houses where Schubert lived. He lived here in 1822/23 with his friend Franz von Schober, writing, amongst other things, his *Unfinished Symphony (symphony in B minor)* and *Die schöne Müllerin*, a work that reflects his own personal crisis at the time, the result of a serious syphilis infection.
1st District, Singerstrasse 28, the "Zu den 3 Hacken" Tavern. Schubert, who never married, frequently met his friends in coffee houses and taverns, including the old 17th century establishment "Zu den 3 Hacken", frequented also by the writers Ferdinand Raimund and Johann Nestroy. The beautiful old Viennese tavern still stands.
6th District, Kettenbrückengasse 6, the house in which Schubert died. Schubert spent the last month of his life in his brother Ferdinand's apartment, dying in 1828 of "nervous fever" (probably typhoid fever). The room in which he died is now a commemorative room.
18th District, Währinger Strasse/Teschnergasse, Schubert Park. Schubert was buried at the former Währing Local Cemetery in the presence of his friends in 1828. The expenses were paid by his brother Ferdinand (the key for the commemorative grove is available free of charge at the nearby office from Mondays to Fridays, 7.00–15.00).

Johann Strauss Monument in the Stadtpark.

11th District, Central Cemetery, Group 32A, Grave No. 28. When the Währing Local Cemetery was abandoned in 1888, Franz Schubert's mortal remains were transferred to an honorary grave at the Central Cemetery, which had been laid out in 1874. The new tombstone is by Carl Kundmann and the Ringstrasse architect Theophil Hansen.
1st District, Stadtpark, Schubert memorial. This memorial, its pedestal by Theophil Hansen and the seated figure of Schubert by Carl Kundmann, was unveiled in 1872.

Johann Strauss the Younger
Strauss (1825–1899) is the undisputed genius of light music, that typical Viennese music of the 19th century best described by the words "waltz" and "operetta". A type of music whose history was largely determined by the Strauss family for over 100 years, by Johann Strauss the Elder and by his sons Josef, Eduard and particularly Johann.
The young Johann had become a musician against his famous father's wishes, and as a 19-year-old created a sensation at his first public performance in 1844 at Dommayer's Casino in Hietzing (today the Park Hotel Schönbrunn). This was the start of his unstoppable ascent to the "Waltz King". Strauss developed the Viennese Biedermeier dance, whose initial success was due to his father, into a concert waltz for symphony orchestra, and his tours through the whole of Europe and North America made him famous around the world. After his father died in 1849, he took over the latter's orchestra, and was designated Imperial Ball Director in 1863. Until 1870, he directed all the Imperial Balls and dedicated himself exclusively to the composition of dance music. Finally, encouraged by Jacques Offenbach, he turned to operetta. *Die Fledermaus*, first performed in 1873 in the Theater an der Wien and also part of the Imperial Opera House's repertoire from 1894, made Johann Strauss the creator of the Viennese operetta at a stroke. The successful Viennese composer was also admired by representatives of classical music. Richard Wagner called him the "most musical skull of the 19th century", and Johannes Brahms wrote on the music of the Blue Danube Waltz, "unfortunately not by me". Strauss wrote 15 operettas, including masterpieces such as *A Night in Venice* (1883) and *The Gypsy Baron* (1885), one opera and 145 waltzes including *Tales from the Vienna Woods* (1868), *Vienna Blood* (1871) and *The Blue Danube* (1867), *the* epitome of the Viennese waltz and the work that rings in every New Year in Austria.

Selected Strauss addresses
2nd District, Praterstrasse 54, Johann Strauss Museum. The house where Strauss was living in 1867 when he wrote *The Blue Danube Waltz* is today the Strauss museum.
6th District, Linke Wienzeile 6, Theater an der Wien. It was here that *Die Fledermaus* was first performed in 1874. This was shortly after the Vienna Stock Exchange crashed, and consequently its first success was achieved in Berlin. Today it is the world's most frequently performed operetta, and is acknowledged as having the

quality of an opera. Strauss's first operetta, *Indigo and the 40 Thieves*, was also first performed in this theatre in 1871, as was *The Gypsy Baron* (1885).

4th District, Johann-Strauss-Gasse 4. In what was then the Igelgasse, Strauss had a palace constructed from 1876 to 1878, and lived there from 1878 until his death in 1899, first in an unhappy marriage with the singer Angelika (Lilly) Dittrich, and then with his third wife Adele Deutsch. The so called "Strauss evenings" brought together the major figures of artistic and cultural life of the time, including Brahms, Bruckner and Puccini. The "Strauss Palace" was destroyed by bombs in 1944, and today a new building stands in its place. The street was renamed the Johann-Strauss-Gasse in the year of Strauss's death, 1899. A mosaic on Nos. 10–14 recalls *The Blue Danube Waltz*, Strauss's most popular composition.

11th District, Central Cemetery, Group 32A, Grave No. 27. This is the grave of honour of Johann Strauss the Younger.

1st District, Stadtpark, Johann Strauss Monument. Strauss as the world remembers him: as the "Waltz King" with his violin. Strauss directed his orchestra while standing and playing his violin, practically his personal trademark.

World famous ambassadors of Viennese music

The Vienna Philharmonic Orchestra

The fact that Vienna is still today regarded as the world capital of music is due not least to the fame of the Vienna Philharmonic Orchestra, one of the world's best orchestras and *the* city's musical visiting card. There is hardly any major event in Vienna for which they do not provide the music, hardly any world tour that does not hit the headlines.

The tradition of the Vienna Philharmonic Orchestra dates back to 1842. It was then that the first leader of the Imperial Opera House Orchestra, the Prussian Otto Nicolai, decided to give regular concerts of exclusively symphonic works with the orchestra. The profits were divided amongst the musicians. In 1870 the orchestra moved into the newly constructed Musikvereinsgebäude (Building of the Music Association) and since then has played in the famous Golden Hall with its 2,000 seats and its perfect acoustics. It is also from here that its legendary New Years Concert with all the most wonderful melodies of Viennese music is broadcast around the world, to an audience of more than one billion.

Today, the Philharmonic Orchestra consists of 140 musicians, who are also members of the State Opera House Orchestra; formerly an exclusive male preserve, its rules have permitted women since 1997 – after more than just a little hesitation. In contrast, there has been no disputing the tradition that the "Viennese" should always be directed by famous conductors, who have included Hans Richter and Gustav Mahler, Wilhelm Furtwängler, Clemens Krauss, Karl Böhm and Herbert von Karajan – some of this century's most brilliant conductors.

The Vienna Boy's Choir

Another institution of Viennese musical life is the famous Boy's Choir, in which Joseph Haydn and Franz Schubert began their careers. The clear sound of this vocal phenomenon has been heard for half a millennium, ever since Emperor Maximilian I established both the Imperial Orchestra and the "Chapel Boy's Choir" in 1498. The latter were responsible for the singing during Mass (depending on the taste of the age, in Dutch style, then Italian and later Classical Viennese style), since women

The Vienna Boy's Choir in the chapel of the Imperial Palace.

were forbidden from participating in liturgical music. This was the birth of what is today the "Vienna Boy's Choir", which has been based in the Baroque Augarten Palais since 1948. It is from here that the choir sets off on its countless tours that conquer the hearts of the audiences around the world. In addition to a general education, the "Golden Voices" also receive comprehensive training in singing and musical theory. Recently, girls have also been admitted to the kindergarten attached to the choir. Members of the choir have to leave when their voices break, but can remain in what is known as the "Mutantenstöckl" (Mutants block) in the Augarten Palais and attend a public school.

Since 1935 there have always been four choirs, one of which performs at Mass on Sundays and holidays at the Imperial Palace Chapel, while the others are available for concerts, tours, films, recordings etc. Mass in the Imperial Palace Chapel is without doubt one of the classical highlights of Viennese musical life. In the strict Gothic setting of the Chapel, the solemn celebration is accompanied by the immortal melodies of the greatest composers played by members of the Vienna Philharmonic Orchestra accompanied by the Vienna Boy's Choir together with singers from the State Opera Chorus.

The Opera Ball, Vienna's most famous event during the carnival period.

After Dark...

Waltzing time

An experience of the very best kind that can only be found in this city is a thrilling ball night during the Viennese ball season. The rustling of taffeta and silk gowns, black dress coats with stiff shirt front, the clinking of glasses of Champagne and the sounds of the waltzes of Lanner and Strauss – just as in the old days, thousands flock to the Viennese balls during the Carnival. The social highlight each year is the *Opera Ball*, for many the ball of all balls, for others the night of mere illusions, commemorating (since 1956) in waltz time the sugar-sweet memories of the imperial glories – all under the spotlight of the media, and practically a state event. The Honorary Chairman is the Austrian Federal President, the Honorary Presidial Council is the Federal Government, the boxes swarm with celebrities from the field of politics, economics and culture, all stand for the national anthem and the European anthem, the State Opera Ballet provides the interludes and the whole glamorous event is watched by millions on television. On the last Thursday before Ash Wednesday, the Vienna State Opera House becomes the most beautiful and most expensive ballroom in the world for 7,000 guests, with flowers flown in specially from the Riviera. The event is formally opened by the State Opera Ballet accompanied by roughly 190 pairs of debutants, after which comes the magic call "Alles Walzer!" (Ladies and Gentlemen the waltz), the signal for everyone to take to the floor. There is music and dancing throughout the whole building. Around 10 orchestras and soloists, including big band and disco sound, play from the cellar up to the gallery. But the ball's speciality has and always will be the Viennese waltz, performed by the Opera Ball Orchestra founded in 1982, a dance that is

the essential element of the glamour of a formal and elegant ball night.
The *Life Ball* has become a completely different type of permanent institution, a glittering and extremely popular event in favour of AIDS charities, and takes place in the Town Hall each May under the auspices of an international couturier and with the assistance of many other famous celebrities. Every year the event is attended by thousands, and over the years it has acquired the status of a cult, adding a new and cosmopolitan facet to the tradition of the classical Viennese ball.

Vienna by Night

The steep alley is lined by one bar after another, every evening the crowds swarm up the hill and back down again. Gathering outside the open doors through which music booms. In summer, Rabensteig and Ruprechtsplatz are a mass of street cafés. This is the *Bermuda Triangle* in the 1st District, the very centre of Vienna's tourist night life, and 20 years ago the birthplace of today's famous night life scene in Vienna. It all began in the 1970s. The work on the No. 1 underground line had just been finished and the somewhat seedy

"Alles Walzer!" are the words that announce that the floor is open to the public at the Opera Ball.

district with its heavily guarded synagogues and the ancient Ruprechtskirche, was being renovated. Suddenly, a completely new trend was started by pioneering establishments such as the *Krah Krah* beer bar or the former *Rote Engel*, now called *Der neue Engel* after a change of ownership at the end of the 1990s. And since then it is here, in the network formed by the Rabensteig, Seitenstettengasse and Ruprechtsplatz, that night-time gastronomy is concentrated. The old-established addresses such as *Ma Pitom* (Hebrew for "suddenly why"), a large restaurant serving Italian and international specialities, or the supreme *Salzamt* with its bar and fine restaurant (designed by Hermann Czech), have been joined by countless other venues. This maze of bars and restaurants may have lost some of its shine in the eyes of the Viennese, but still continues to flourish thanks above all to its legendary reputation amongst visitors to Vienna. At the same time newcomers continue to refresh its image, such as the lively Caribbean *Ron con soda* (70 types of rum) or the *First Floor* upstairs, one of the most attractive cocktail bars in the city. To get a picture of the variety of nightly activities in this area, there is no alternative to setting off on the trail yourself. But such a pub tour isn't entirely without danger, for many a visitor is said to have been temporarily lost in the depths of these old city alleys, having forgotten all about going home – hence the name. It was in the 1980s, when the area was turning into the night-life district, that it was suddenly dubbed the Bermuda Triangle. This had been an in-expression from the previous decade, when the first bars began to gather around the Naschmarkt – the seeds of today's widespread and multifarious bar scene that has now become an attraction for an international public.

In the "First Floor" bar.

It was also at this time that the first in-bars were being opened in the inner city, where they have continued to boom: the *Kleine Café* on Franziskanerplatz or the *Wunderbar* in Schönlaterngasse (both fitted out by the architect Hermann Czech). Now there are numerous other Bermuda Triangles in Vienna, with in-venues side by side, frequented by a regular commuter traffic. These include the district around Bäckerstrasse with the ancient *Alt Wien*, the celebrity bar *Oswald & Kalb* or the *Café Engländer* with its bar and restaurant, as well as countless other bars and pubs for all ages in the adjoining districts (Schönlaterngasse, Sonnenfelsgasse etc.). The clientele in the quarter around Rudolfsplatz is somewhat younger, forming queues in front of the "colonial" *Planter's Club*, spilling over into the *Oskar* or the *Häfn* or the fashionable *Apropos*. The Spittelberg, with the vast *Plutzer-Bräu*, the *Lux*, the *Amerlingbeisl* or the *Objektiv*, has also become a type of Bermuda Triangle. Another in-area is the district around Schottenfeldgasse, Richtergasse and Zollergasse in the 7th District, with the *Blue Box* or the *Pulse* setting the trend in the field of current DJ culture, while the *Europa*, a permanent fixture in the Viennese bar scene, is less particular about the age of its clientele. And around the Naschmarkt and Schleifmühlgasse there are establishments such as the *Amacord* (for excellent meals and good music) the Brasileiro bar *Saci* at Mühlgasse 20 (downstairs a bar, upstairs a Brazilian restaurant), around the corner from the *Café Anzengruber*, an artists' café since the end of the last century, with

billiards, draught Budweiser (the Czech variety) and excellent Wiener Schnitzel, or the bright and spacious *Freihaus*, and many more.
In contrast, the more central streets around the Kärntner Strasse contain the more expensive clubs. Here are the *Moulin Rouge* and the *Eden Bar*, the *Casanova Revue Bar* in Dorotheergasse, the

Champagne establishment *Reiss-Bar*, the famous and tiny *Loos-Bar (American Bar)* or the 2 storey cocktail bar *New York, New York*. Generally the city has seen a boom in bars, a trend that started from the hotel-bar *Barfly's* owned by Mario Castillo, the proprietor of a growing number of bars in Vienna. No-one knows exactly when and how the somewhat rigid and sleepy post-war Vienna metamorphosed into today's mercurial and racy metropolis for night-life lovers. There is no doubt that this development was aided by the fact that Vienna has the most liberal opening hour regulations in the German speaking world alongside Berlin. Vienna has become fashionable, not least because of this boom. Today there are over 6,000 establishments in the city, easily enabling those who never sleep to put together a 24 hour programme. For this reason, it is only possible to make a small selection from the wide variety available to those who like going out and turning night into day. The list of in-bars never stops growing and changing, with some disappearing or becoming insignificant, and it has long been impossible to list all of them anyway – the best thing is to follow the crowds, look in, see for oneself, try the place, find a few companions and lose them again …

Clubbing in the Gasometer in Simmering.

Following page: View of the Leopold Wing of the Imperial Palace, in the background St. Stephen's Cathedral.

VIENNA TIPS

The best music festivals

Resonanzen. Performances of classical music on different themes each year in the Vienna Konzerthaus (January).

Haydn-Tage. With focus on aspects on the works of Haydn; events in the Wiener Musikverein and in churches (March).

OsterKlang. Classical festival in the week before Easter with top quality events in the sumptuous concert halls and selected venues (April).

International Music Festival of the Vienna Festival Weeks. A highlight of the Viennese concert year (May–June).

Jazzfest Wien. International jazz celebrities in the State Opera House, the Volksoper and in jazz clubs (July).

KlangBogen – Vienna Musical Summer. Orchestral concerts, opera and operetta performances cast a network of sound over the whole city (July–August).

Mozart in Schönbrunn. Open-air performances of Mozart's operas in the Schönbrunn Palace Park in front of the Roman Ruins (July–August).

Music Film Festival. Open-air event on the Town Hall Square presenting famous orchestras and conductors; admission free (July–August).

Wien Modern. Series of events involving 20th century classical music, founded by Claudio Abbado (October–November).

Wiener Schubertiade. Series of events in the Wiener Musikverein presenting works by Schubert (November).

The most beautiful religious music

Augustinerkirche. High Mass with music by the choir of St. Augustin's, Sundays 11.00; July, August, organ mass; Fridays 19.30, various concerts.

Imperial Palace Chapel. Mass with the Vienna Imperial Orchestra with the Vienna Boy's Choir, the Vienna Philharmonic and singers from the State Opera, September–June, Sundays 9.15.

Michaelerkirche. Various concert performances, as well as organ concerts on Vienna's largest Baroque organ during the first two weeks of October.

Minoritenkirche. Concert events and Masses with music.

Schottenkirche. Religious music one evening per month; June and December, organ and trumpet music; meditative organ music during Lent daily from 17.15 to 17.45; admission free

Stephansdom. High Mass with music, September–June, Sundays 10.15, July and August at 9.15; as well as occasional concert events; particularly recommendable is Christmas music on December 24, at 16.30 (Mozart), as well as Christmas carols and brass music from the tower before and during Midnight Mass at 24.00; High Mass on December 25 with choral and orchestral works by the Viennese classical composers among others (for more information about the cathedral and its music, see under <http://st-stephan.or.at/>).

Jesuitenkirche. Classical orchestra mass, September–June, Sundays 10.00

Votivkirche. There is an organ festival at the beginning of September each year; church music (choir and orchestra) in Advent and Lent and on religious holidays; also frequent concerts by commercial organisers.

The best music venues

The Vienna State Opera House. Operas, ballet, in summer a venue of the Vienna Jazz Festival; performances from September to June.

Vienna Volksoper. Operas, operettas, musicals, ballet; performances from September to June.

Vienna Chamber Opera House. Operas, Singspiel; performances October–June, Mondays, Wednesdays, Saturdays, 19.30; in July and August performances in the Schönbrunn Palace Theatre and in the Palace Park.

Theater an der Wien. Musicals, guest performances, concerts, dance; performances Thursdays–Tuesdays, 19.30; Sundays 18.00 (not all year round).

Raimundtheater. Musicals, comedies; performances Thursdays–Sundays, 19.30.

Musikverein – Gesellschaft der Musikfreunde in Wien. The New Year's Concert by the Vienna Philharmonic Orchestra in the large Musikvereinssaal, and a great deal more besides; performances September–June, concerts begin at 19.30.

Vienna Konzerthaus. Concert events of all kinds, one of the most important venues for contemporary music, including jazz; performances all year round, no specific starting times.

Arnold Schönberg Centre. Concerts, exhibitions and other events; the composer's entire estate.

Bösendorfer Saal. Primarily guest performances, mostly piano music; performances September–June, 19.30.

Ronacher. Once the greatest variety theatre stage in the city, today a private theatre for all kinds of guest performances (musicals, variety theatre, etc.).

The best specialist museums

Bestattungsmuseum (Funeral Museum). 4th District, Goldeggasse 19, Tel. 501 95-22 007. Can be visited only by prior appointment and only on a guided tour, Mondays–Fridays 12.00–15.00.

Biedermeier Museum Geymüller-Schlössel. 18th District, Khevenhüllerstrasse 2, Tel. 479 31 39, March–November Thursdays–Sundays 10.00–17.00, guided tours Sundays, 15.00.

Circus- and Clownmuseum (Austrian Circus and Clown Museum). 2nd District, Karmelitergasse 9, Tel. 211 06-021 27, Wednesdays 17.30–19.00, Saturdays 14.30–17.00, Sundays 10.00–12.00.

Feuerwehrmusuem (Fire Brigade Museum). 1st District, Am Hof 7; Tel. 531 99; Sundays and public holidays, 9.00–12.00, workdays by prior appointment by telephone

Kriminalmuseum (Museum of Crime). 2nd District, Grosse Sperlgasse 24; Tel. 214 46 78; daily except Mondays unless public holidays, 10.00–17.00

Lipizzaner Museum. 1st District, Reitschulgasse 2, Tel. 526 41 84-30, daily 9.00–18.00.

Puppen- und Spielzeugmuseum (Doll and Toy Museum). 1st District, Schulhof 4, Tel. 535 68 60, Tuesdays–Sundays 10.00–18.00.

Österreichisches Theatermuseum (Austrian Theatre Museum). 1st District, Lobkowitzplatz 2, Tel. 512 88 00-0, Tuesdays–Sundays 10.00–17.00; Children's Theatre Museum, Tuesdays–Sundays, 10.00–17.00.

Uhrenmuseum der Stadt Wien (Clock Museum of the City of Vienna). 1st District, Schulhof 2, Tel. 533 22 65, Tuesdays–Sundays 9.00–16.30.

Vienna Tramway Museum. 3rd district, Ludwig Koessler Platz; Tel. 79 09-449 00; beginning of May–October, Saturdays, Sundays, public holidays, 9.00–16.00

Interesting Vienna Galleries

Ariadne. Main interest: younger artists particularly in the fields of painting and drawing (Peter Pongratz, Hubert Schmalix, Jeannot Schwarz etc.). 1st district, Bäckerstrasse 6; Tel. 512 94 79; Tuesdays–Fridays 13.00–18.00, Thursdays 13.00–20.00, Saturdays 10.00–13.00

Heike Curtze. Contemporary art, particularly the first post-war generation (C.L. Attersee, G. Brus, M. Lassnig, H. Nitsch) and Art Brut artists (J. Hauser, O. Tschirtner, A. Walla) from the Gugging psychiatric hospital (near Vienna). 1st district, Seilerstätte 15; Tel. 512 93 75; Tuesdays –Fridays 11.00–18.00, Saturdays 11.00–14.00

Faber Austrian and Czech photography, historical and modern (Inge Dick, Trude Fleischmann, Vilem Reichmann etc.). 4th district, Brahmsplatz 7; Tel. 505 75 18; Tuesdays–Fridays 14.00–18.00, Saturdays 10.00–13.00

Hilger. Classical modern (Pablo Picasso, Jean

Dubuffet etc.) and Austrians (A. Hrdlicka, O. Oberhuber, etc.). 1st district, Dorotheergasse 5; Tel. 512 53 15; Tuesdays–Fridays 12.00–18.00 Saturdays 10.00–13.00
Grita Insam. Austrian avantgarde (B. Kowanz, F. Pichler, M. Wakolbinger, P. Weibl etc.), plenty of experimental media art (videos, installations). 1st district, Kölnerhofgasse 6; Tel. 512 53 30; Tuesdays–Fridays 12.00–18.00, Saturdays 11.00–14.00
Hummel. Actionists and Jugendstil, thematic exhibitions (B. Gironcoli, B. Kowanz, O. Mühl, H. Nitsch, A. Rainer, F. West etc.). 1st district, Bäckerstrasse 14; Tel. 512 12 96; Tuesdays–Fridays 15.00–18.00, Saturdays 10.00–13.00
Krinzinger. Activities include large exhibitions by the artists represented by the gallery (P. Kogler, E. Schlegel, H. Schmalix, E. Wurm etc.), as well as thematic exhibitions often accompanied by symposia. 1st district, Seilerstätte 16; Tel. 513 30 06; Tuesdays–Fridays 12.00–18.00, Saturdays 10.00–13.00
Nächst St. Stephan. One of the most important centres of contemporary Austrian avantgarde. 1st district, Grünangergasse 1; Tel. 512 12 66; Mondays–Fridays 11.00–18.00, Saturdays 11.00–14.00
Ulysses. Above all abstract Austrians and Americans (B. Gironcoli, H. Hollein, K. Kogelnig, M. Lassnig, H. Nitsch, A. Rainer, F. Wotruba etc.). 1st district, Opernring 21; Tel. 587 12 26; Tuesdays–Fridays 10.00–18.00, Saturdays 10.00–13.00

The Customer is Emperor!

Many of the businesses that acquired the much sought-after title of "Imperial and Royal Supplier to the Court" during the monarchy, still exist, offering their customers a combination of top quality and a particular flair.
Joh. Backhausen & Söhne. Home textiles. Furnishers of the Ringstrasse buildings. Designs by Jugendstil artists still used today. 1st District, Kärntner Strasse. 33
E. Bakalowits & Söhne. Chandeliers, glass and porcelain. 1st District, Spiegelgasse 3
L. Bösendorfer. World-famous piano manufacturers with a list of customers ranging from Franz List to Leonard Bernstein. 1st District, Canovagasse 4
Ch. Demel's Söhne. Legendary court confectioners, whose products decorated the imperial Christmas tree and were served at court balls. 1st District, Kohlmarkt 14
Gerstner. Court confectioners, Café-Konditorei, restaurant. 1st District, Kärntner Strasse 15
Kattus. Once the world's largest caviar dealer, today still a producer and importer of sparkling wines. 19th District, Silbergasse 52
A. E. Köchert. Court jewellers and the imperial family's personal goldsmith. 1st District, Neuer Markt 15
Kniže & Comp. Elegant men's outfitters, today also supplying ladies' fashions. 1st District, Graben 13
J. & L. Lobmeyr. Court glassware supplier; many of these imperial services can be seen today in the Imperial Silver and Tableware Chamber. 1st District, Kärntner Strasse 26
Wiener Porzellanmanufaktur Augarten. Exquisite porcelain, hand-painted, the second oldest porcelain manufacturer in Europe. 1st District, Stock-im-Eisen-Platz 3–4. 6th District, Mariahilferstrasse 99.

The most attractive coffee-houses

Bräunerhof. Once the writer Thomas Bernhard's regular café; with plenty of newspapers and good desserts. Chamber music at weekends. 1st District, Stallburggasse 2.
Central. Very elegant and attractive coffeehouse. 1st District, Herrengasse 14.
Eiles. A café with a long-standing tradition near the Town Hall and Parliament, also serving meals. 8th District, Josephstädter Strasse 2.
Griensteidl. Very large and popular coffee-house near the Hofburg. 1st District, Michaelerplatz 2.
Hawelka. The traditional haunt of artists; speciality of the house: Mrs. Hawelka's Buchteln (hot small buns filled with jam). 1st District, Dorotheergasse 6.
Landtmann. An old splendid Ringstrasse café with celebrities from politics and culture. Meals all day long. A larger sunny terrace facing the Burgtheater. 1st District, Dr. Karl Luegerring 4.
Museum. Originally constructed by Adolf Loos; a very popular café with chess room, television and tables for games that the guests bring with them. 1st District, Friedrichstrasse 6.
Prückel. It's clear from the menu that the service has not changed since the days of the Habsburg Monarchy! Magnificent 1950s atmosphere. Regulars mainly intellectuals. Bridge in the back room. 1st District, Stubenring 24.
Ritter. Large coffee-house with a view of the hustle and bustle on the Mariahilfer Strasse. With bridge, chess and a guest garden. 6th District, Mariahilfer Strasse 73.
Sperl. One of the oldest coffee-houses, near the Naschmarkt, completely refurbished in the 1980s. Still very popular with billiards, chess and bridge. Small garden. 6th District, Gumpendorfer Strasse 11.

The markets

The markets of Vienna provide excellent hands-on local colour combined with the opportunity of getting a souvenir or two. In addition to the numerous food markets such as the **Karmelitermarkt** or the **Naschmarkt**, it is above all the Christmas markets that are the most traditional. The most popular and largest is the Christkindl Market in front of the **town hall**, with its countless sales stands and snack bars, the decorated trees in the park and an old Viennese post office with Christmas stamps and special postmark (mid November–December 24; daily 9.00–21.00; on December 24, 9.00–17.00). The streets of the picturesque district of **Spittelberg** each year host the atmospheric Spittelberg Christmas Market with its stands of handicraft goods (November 20–December 23, Mondays–Fridays 14.00–20.00, Saturdays, Sundays 10.00–20.00). The Culture and Christmas Market in **Schönbrunn** occupies a magnificent setting. The Baroque main courtyard of the Palace is the scene of this delightful Advent market with its numerous handicraft Christmas presents, accompanied by the sounds of daily music concerts. Other popular Christmas markets with plenty of character are to be found in the 1st District on the **Freyung** (there is also an Easter market here) and in the **Heiligenkreuzer Hof** (only Saturdays and Sundays), and in front of the Karlskirche (4th District). The Vienna art and antiquities markets have for years been popular amongst connoisseurs, collectors and anyone who loves digging around. The Art and Antiques Market extends along the **Danube Canal Promenade** between the Schwedenplatz and Schottenring underground stations (May–September, Saturdays afternoons). There is a similar market on the Am Hof square (1st District) (March–Christmas, Fridays, Saturdays 10.00–19.00). Art and craft goods are available at the Art Market on the Spittelberg every Saturday from 10.00–18.00. However, the Flea Market at the **Naschmarkt** is an absolute must for bargain hunters and strollers. Every Saturday from 6 o'clock in the morning until the afternoon, the market is crowded with buyers, experts and the just plain curious (Kettenbrückengasse U4 underground station). Everything imaginable and unimaginable can be found here, from genuine antiques, old books and records, clothes and crockery to the most unbelievable junk. Together with the Naschmarkt, the Flea Market represents a total Viennese experience that should not be missed.

Vienna from above – the best viewpoints of the city

St. Stephen's Tower (south tower). 343 steps to a unique view over Vienna
Haas Haus. The best view of the "Steffl" from the Do & Co restaurant
Belvedere Palace Park. A magnificent panorama of Vienna from the Upper Belvedere

Schönbrunn Palace Park. A magnificent panorama of the city from the Gloriette
Ferris Wheel in the Prater. Still one of Vienna's landmarks with a view
Windows of Vienna. Vienna's highest restaurant, on the 22nd storey. 10th District, Wienerbergstrasse 7
Danube Tower in the Danube Park. 252 m high, Vienna's tallest building; with a viewing terrace (150 m) and two revolving restaurants at 160 and 170 m. 22nd District, Donauturmstrasse 4
Salettl Pavilion. Old Viennese "Salettl" (bower) with garden, view of the Vienna Woods. 19th District, Hartäckerstrasse 80
Kahlenberg. One of Vienna's local hills, the classic tour for a view
Jubiläumswarte (Jubilee Tower). This panorama tower provides a wonderful view over Vienna. 16th District, next to Johann-Staud-Strasse 80

The most attractive country inns

Tiroler Garten. Tavern in the style of a Tyrolean mountain hut in the heart of the Schönbrunn Palace Park, next to an alpine zoo for children. 13th District, Schönbrunn Palace Park/Tyrolean Garden; Tel. 879 38 03; daily 11.00–23.00.
Schloss Wilhelminenberg. Constructed in 1785 as the summer palace for a prince, the building was later altered on several occasions, finally being converted into a hotel and restaurant in 1988. An excellent view of Vienna from the large terrace. 16th District, Savoyenstrasse 2; Tel. 485 85 03; daily 11.00–23.00
Cobenzl. Popular café terrace with a somewhat faded elegance, but a magnificent view of Vienna. Am Cobenzl 94; Tel. 320 51 20; daily 11.30–22.00
Häuserl am Stoan. Romantic forest tavern on the panorama road with a view of Vienna. 19th District, Zierleitengasse 42a; Tel. 440 13 77; Mondays–Sundays 11.00–24.00
Hotel Restaurant Sophienalpe. A popular destination for shorter tours in the Vienna Woods; children's playground! Sophienalpe 13; Tel. 486 24 32-0; daily 7.00–24.00; in winter only Saturdays and Sundays
Rohrhaus. Tavern with garden and children's playground in the Lainz Animal Reserve; April–October, Wednesdays–Sundays.
Grilisauer. Old Viennese tavern with a beautiful garden. 14th District, Linzerstrasse 423; Tel. 979 32 28; Tuesdays 16.00–24.00, Wednesdays–Sundays, 9.00–24.00
Zur alten Kaisermühle. Popular destination directly on the Old Danube, famous for its spare ribs and fish specialities. Reserve a table and bring insect protection in the evenings. 21st District, Old Danube, Fischerstrand 21a; Tel. 263 35 29; end of April–middle of September, daily 11.30–23.00
Lindmayer. Attractive Danube restaurant directly on the river, famous for its fish specialities. 2nd District, Dammhaufen 50; Tel. 728 95 80; Tuesdays–Sundays 10.00–21.00, closed Mondays except public holidays
Zum Roten Hiasl. Best-known, very folkloristic tavern in the Lobau. Am Schutzdamm 128 (Industriestrasse/Biberhaufenweg); Tel. 280 71 22; daily 9.00–24.00

Vienna for the romantic – secluded alleys, hidden bars and cafés, idyllic spots

In the tranquil garden of the Kleine Café on the **Franziskanerplatz**, you can dream away a whole summer's afternoon in the heart of the hustle and bustle of the city.
Zu ebener Erde und erster Stock. A delightful restaurant in a Biedermeier dolls' house, named after a play by Johann Nestroy. The first floor contains the pink room, with wooden beamed ceiling, curtains and excellent cuisine. 7th District, Burggasse 13; Tel. 523 62 54; Mondays–Saturdays, 12.00–14.30, 18.00–23.30
A park bench in the **Volksgarten** (1st District), when the roses are in blossom and the air is full of their scent, is a good place for holding hands.
Discothek Gerard. Secluded cocktail bar with a small dance floor (soul, funk, dance-floor), sumptuous and decadent in style, no doubt due to the red lamp that once decorated the entrance. 8th District, Lederergasse 11; Tel. 402 07 86; daily 20.00–4.00
Feel yourself transported back into bygone Vienna by the sounds of the "Wiener Walzermädchen" Ladies Orchestra in the summer garden of the **Café Dommayer** at Schönbrunn.
A walk from Grinzing along the Himmelstrasse to the **Am Himmel** and **Bellevue Höhe** area.
Hans Sirbu Heurige. A picturesque spot in the heart of vineyards, high above the city, with the most magnificent view from any Heurige over Vienna and the Danube. 19th District, Kahlenberger Strasse 210; Tel. 320 59 28; April–October, daily 15.00–24.00
Laxenburg Palace. Boating with character – drifting across the quiet palace pond, letting your mind wander.
New Year's Eve on the **Spittelberg** in the snow, welcoming the New Year by candle-light and torches instead of the sound of fireworks.
The view from the **Kahlenberg** on Vienna by night.

Viennese Beisl – in all variations

Reinthaler. Genuine Beisl in a central location with a garden 1., Gluckgasse 5; Tel. 512 33 66; Mondays–Thursdays 9–23, Friday 9.00–16.00
Zu den 3 Hacken. Cosy Viennese establishment; a classic in the heart of the city. 1., Singerstraße 28; Tel. 512 58 95; Mondays–Saturdays 9.00–24.00
Zum Alten Heller. Higher-quality homely establishment; attractive garden and excellent Schnitzel. 3., Ungargasse 34; Tel. 712 64 52; Tuesdays–Saturdays 9.30–23.00 (warm meals 11.30–14.00, 17.30–22.00)
Rudi's Beisl. Small popular Beisl well known for its good home cooking. 5., Wiedner Hauptstraße 88; Tel. 544 51 02; Mondays–Fridays 12.30–15.30, 18.00–24.00
Zur Goldenen Glocke. The tap room is a traditional Beisl with upper-quality Viennese cuisine. Extremely popular garden with wall frescos. 5., Schönnbrunner Straße 8; Tel. 587 57 67; Mondays–Saturdays 11.00–14.30, 17.30–24.00
Grünauer. Sophisticated Beisl with gourmet ambitions and an excellent wine list. 7., Hermanngasse 32; Tel. 526 40 80; Mondays 18.00–24.00, Tuesdays–Fridays 11.30–15.00, 18.00–24.00
Wegenstein. Long-standing Beisl with a wide mix of guests. 7., Lerchenfelder Straße 73; Tel. 526 78 72; Mondays–Fridays 8.00–24.00, Saturdays 9.00–14.00
Gasthaus Wickerl. Excellent Upper Austrian-Viennese cuisine. 9., Porzellangasse 24a; Tel. 317 74 89; Mondays–Fridays, public holidays 8.00–24.00, Saturdays 8.00–14.00 Uhr

In-venues

Der neue Engel. once a pioneer of the legendary Bermuda Triangle, fitted out by the Coop Himmelb(l)au group of architects, now devoted to the cities of Vienna, Dublin, Sidney, Shanghai and Cairo in terms of alcohol and videos. 1st District, Rabensteig 5; Tel. 535 41 05; Mondays–Wednesdays 16.00–2.00, Thursdays, Fridays 16.00–3.00, Saturdays, Sundays 18.00–3.00.
Krah Krah. One of Vienna's most famous beer establishments, jazz on Sunday mornings, over 50 types of beer and huge black-bread sandwiches. 1st District, Rabensteig 8, Tel. 533 81 93; daily 11.00–2.00
Oskar. Viennese cooking all day until 24.00; young in-crowd; part of the Rudolfsplatz scene, 1st District, Concordiaplatz 2; Tel. 533 83 55; Mondays–Thursdays 11.00–2.00, Fridays 11.00–4.00, Saturdays 18.00–4.00, Sundays 18.00–2.00.
Häfn. Always full, slightly earthy, but ideal for flirting; part of the Rudolfsplatz scene. 1st District, Gonzagagasse 12; Tel. 535 02 82; Mondays–Thursdays 18.00–4.00, Saturdays 18.00–5.00.
Bane's Bar. Popular stand-up bar with good food, also the meeting point for English speakers; the closing time is usually dealt with

generously; On the edge of the Bäckerstrasse scene. 1st District, Köllnerhofgasse 3; Tel. 512 02 79; Mondays–Fridays 12.00–4.00, Saturdays, Sundays 20.00–4.00.
Café Alt Wien. The intellectual and artist scene made this establishment a legend in the early 1980s; mostly students. 1st District, Bäckerstrasse 9; Tel. 512 52 22; Sundays–Thursdays 10.00–2.00, Fridays, Saturdays 10.00–4.00.
Oswald & Kalb. Major meeting point of the cultural glitterati; classic tavern food in ancient vaults; attractive dark panelled bar room. 1st District, Bäckerstrasse 14; Tel. 512 13 71; daily 18.00–2.00.
Enrico Panigl. Small Italian wine bar with music, crowds and good food. 1st District, Schönlaterngasse 11; Tel. 513 17 16; Mondays–Fridays 18.00–4.00, Saturdays, Sundays, public holidays 20.00–4.00.
Schwimmende Pyramide. Earthy beer bar with hot food until 3.30 or 4.30; 100 types of beer! 1st District, Seilerstätte 3a; Tel. 513 29 70; Sundays–Thursdays 16.00–4.00, Fridays, Saturdays 16.00–5.00.
Marias Roses. Mexican-style bar that is always full; hot tex-mex food until 1.00; a dark salsa disco and show barkeepers in the cellar. 1st District, Biberstrasse 8; Tel. 513 22 21; Tuesdays–Saturdays 18.00–2.00, Sundays, Mondays 18.00–1.00.
Santo Spirito. Small Italienate bar for all ages and lovers of classical music, which is here more than just background noise. 1st District, Kumpfgasse 7; Tel. 512 99 98; daily 10.00–2.00.
Café Stein. Stylistic students' bar occupying two storeys, with an elegant diner in the basement. 9th District, Währinger Strasse 6–8; Tel. 319 72 41; Mondays–Saturdays 7.00–1.00, Sundays 9.00–1.00.
Marias Cantina. The most popular Mexican bar, with tex-mex dishes, a discotheque in the cellar (until 4.00); the predecessor of Marias Roses (see above), but with a younger public. 9th District, Schubertgasse 13; Tel. 310 65 73; daily 18.00–2.00.
Europa. Spacious establishment in 1980s design, a pioneer of the bar scene in this district. 7th District, Zollergasse 8; Tel. 526 33 83; daily 9.00–5.00, excellent meals until 4.00.
Blue Box. A relic from the wild early 1980s, generally young clientele; daily from 20.00, DJ line. 7th District, Richtergasse 8; Tel. 523 26 82; Tuesdays–Sundays 10.00–2.00, Mondays 18.00–2.00.
Pulse. In-bar focusing on innovatory music, good DJ line on Fridays and Saturdays. 7th District, Schottenfeldgasse 3; Tel. 523 60 20; Sundays–Thursdays 18.00–2.00, Fridays, Saturdays 18.00–4.00.

Cocktail bars
Bristol Bar (in the Hotel Bristol). 1st American bar in Vienna, large selection of Austrian spirits and international cocktails; cigars, piano music. 1st District, Mahlerstrasse 2; Tel. 515 16-0; daily 11.00–1.00.
Plato's Retreat. Attractively designed dance bar (designer, Peter Schaberl) in the basement of the Künstlerhaus, belonging to "Noodles & Co" next-door, and managed by the landlady of the Loos-Bar; at times the mix of music is provided by the popular ex-footballer Hans Krankl. 1st District, Karlsplatz 5; Tel. 505 38 39; daily 21.00–5.00
Loos-Bar. Vienna's most attractive bar – small but an absolute must (architect Adolf Loos). 1st District, Kärntner Strasse 10; Tel. 510 32 83; daily 18.00–4.00
Reiss-Bar. Champagne bar with cigars, oysters and celebrities (designed by the Coop Himmelb(l)au architect duo). 1st District, Marco-d'Aviano-Gasse 1; Tel. 512 71 98; Mondays–Fridays 11.00–3.00, Saturdays 10.00–3.00, Sundays 11.00–2.00.
New York, New York. Classic bar occupying two storeys, with music by Frank Sinatra and Co. 1st District, Annagasse 8; Tel. 513 86 51; Mondays–Thursdays 17.00–2.00, Fridays 17.00–3.00, Saturdays 19.00–3.00.
Nightfly's Club. 400 different whiskies and 250 cocktails; cigars. 1st District, Dorotheergasse 14; Tel. 512 99 79; Mondays–Wednesdays 20.00–3.00, Thursdays–Saturdays 20.00–4.00.
First Floor. Top-quality cocktail bar and an example of bar architecture well worth seeing; attraction: a huge aquarium without fish; attractive view (1st floor) of what's going on in the Bermuda Triangle. 1st District, Seitenstettengasse/Rabensteig; Tel. 533 78 66; Mondays–Saturdays 19.00–4.00, Sundays 19.00–3.00.
Rasputin. Stand-up bar with a Russian accent, salmon, caviar and 60 types of vodka; best after midnight. 1st District, Seitenstettengasse 3; Tel. 535 33 87; daily 19.00–4.00.
Broadway Piano Bar. Secluded cocktail bar, sparkling wine, live music, artist's bar; near the Bermuda Triangle. 1st District, Bauernmarkt 21; Tel. 533 28 49; Mondays–Saturdays 21.00–3.00.
Planter's Club. Huge colonial-style bars, top-quality spirits from the Caribbean, Scotland and France, and a humidor for storing cigars – one of the most popular bars in the city, long queues (tip: first eat in the "Livingstone", then there's no problem getting in). 1st District, Zelinkagasse 4; Tel. 533 33 93; daily 17.00–4.00.
Castillo: Stylish in-bar in the Bäckerstrasse district, a classic among the cocktail bars; interesting after midnight. 1st District, Sonnenfelsgasse 9; Tel. 513 14 99; daily 21.00–4.00.
Barfly's Club. Popular American bar in the rear wing of the Hotel Metternich; over 300 types of whisky and over 80 types of rum; the origin of the Castillo empire. 6th District, Esterházygasse 36; Tel. 586 08 25; Mondays–Thursdays 18.00–3.00, Saturdays 18.00–4.00, Sundays 19.00–2.00.

Discotheques
Queen Anne. Chic disco with adjoining cocktail and sparkling-wine bar, evergreens bar; shows and live music on Thursdays. 1st District, Johannesgasse 12; Tel. 512 02 03; Sundays–Thursdays 22.00–4.00, Saturdays 22.00–6.00.
Take Five. The classic quality dance bar. 1st District, Annagasse 3a; Tel. 512 92 77; daily 22.00–4.00.
Montevideo. Trend music, dance floor. 1st District, Annagasse 3; Tel. 512 99 06; Thursdays–Saturdays 23.00–4.00.
P1. Techno, teenies and a few early 20s. 1st District, Rothgasse 9; Tel. 535 99 95; daily 21.00–4.00.
Volksgarten-Disco. Clubbings and scenes changing daily; simply drop in and see what's going on. 1st District, Burgring 1; Tel. 533 05 18; daily 22.00–4.00.
Roxy. From 1960s and 1970s music to soul and dance-floor. 4th District, Operngasse 24; Tel. 587 26 75; daily 22.00–4.00.
Robert Goodman. Starts getting lively around 5 o'clock in the morning on; dancing goes on well into the morning. 4th District, Rechte Wienzeile 23; Tel. 586 34 96; daily 24.00–2.00, 4.00–10.00.
U4. Long-standing but still up-to-date underground disco with music themes changing daily from House to La Notte Italiana. 12th District, Schönbrunner Strasse 222; Tel. 815 83 07; Fridays–Wednesdays 22.00–5.00, Thursdays 23.00–5.00.
Nachtwerk. Vienna's largest disco, attracting thousands of teenagers; on the edge of the city. 23rd District, Dr.-Gonda-Gasse 9; Tel. 616 88 80; Thursdays–Saturdays and the eve of any public holiday 21.00–5.00.
Atoll. Floating open-air summer disco on the Copa Cagrana, excellent for flirting! 22nd District, Donauinsel U3 underground station; Tel. 232 49 59; May–September 19.00–5.00.

Night-clubs, revues and variety clubs
Eden Bar. Elegant meeting place of Viennese society, with live dance music; a Viennese night life institution. 1st District, Liliengasse 2; Tel. 512 74 50; daily 22.00–4.00.
Moulin Rouge. Well-known night-club with dancing, shows and entertainment and plenty of eroticism; also a clubbing address. 1st District, Waalfischgasse 11; Tel. 512 21 30; daily 22.00–6.00.

Maxime Club. Elegant club with Champagne, artistic and erotic show programmes; 3 performances daily. 1st District, Opernring 11; Tel. 586 33 40; Mondays–Fridays 13.00–5.00, Saturdays 21.00–5.00, Sundays 20.00–4.00.
Casanova Revue Bar. Attractive and spacious setting for mostly "family" shows combining artistry with eroticism. 1st District, Dorotheergasse 6–8; Tel. 512 98 45; Mondays–Fridays 12.00–6.00, Saturdays, Sundays 21.00–6.00.

Night life for lesbians and gays

Why not? Night bar and disco (gays/lesbians). 1st District, Tiefer Graben 22, Tel. 535 11 58; Fridays, Saturdays 23.00–4.00, Sundays 21.00–2.00
Café Rainer. Gays. 4th District, Kettenbrückengasse 4; Tel. 586 23 62; daily 21.00–4.00
Arriba. Disco; lesbians. 6th District, Gumpendorfer Strasse 9; Tel. 585 27 26; Fridays from 21.00
Café Willendorf. In the official Rosa Lila Villa information Centre; excellent restaurant with bar for gays, lesbians and heteros. 6th District, Linke Wienzeile 102; Tel. 587 17 89; daily 19.00–2.00
Café Restaurant Orlando. Viennese and international cuisine; lesbian and all others. 6th District, Mollardgasse 3; Tel. 586 23 27; daily 18.00–2.00
Frauencafé. The only café exclusively for women. 8th District, Lange Gasse 11; Tel. 406 37 54; Mondays–Saturdays 18.00–2.00 (closed Mondays and Wednesdays in July and August)
Café Savoy. Sumptuous café; gays and others. 6th District, Linke Wienzeile 36; Tel. 586 73 48; Mondays–Fridays 17.00–2.00, Saturdays 9.00–18.00, 21.00–2.00
Eagle Bar. Leather bar with dark-room, gays. 6th District, Blümelgasse 1; Tel. 587 26 61; daily 21.00–3.00
Café Berg. Elegant café with excellent meals. Gay and lesbian magazines (the adjoining bookshop "Löwenherz" is also interesting); gays, lesbians, heteros. 9th District, Berggasse 8; Tel. 319 57 20; daily 10.00–1.00
U4 Disco. Thursdays from 23.00: Heaven Gay Night; House-Club; also lesbians. 12th District, Schönbrunner Strasse 222; Tel. 815 83 07

Venues for women travelling alone

Restaurant Orlando. 6th District, Mollardgasse 3; Tel. 586 23 27; daily 18.00–2.00
Restaurant Lipizzaner. 1st District, Bräunerstrasse 8; Tel. 533 90 91; daily 11.30–24.00
Neuwien. Restaurant with bar. 1st District, Bäckerstrasse 5; Tel. 513 06 66; daily 18.00–2.00 (meals until 24.00)
First Floor. Cocktail bar. 1st District, Seitenstettengasse/Rabensteig; Tel. 533 78 66; Mondays–Saturdays 19.00–4.00, Sundays 19.00–3.00
Barfly's Club. Cocktail bar. 6th District, Esterh·zygasse 33, Tel. 586 08 25; Mondays–Thursdays 18.00–3.00, Saturdays 18.00–4.00, Sundays 19.00–2.00
Café Lux. Café with international newspapers, bar, excellent meals. 7th District, Schrankgasse 4, Tel. 526 94 91, daily 10.00–2.00
Hotel Stefanie. Café-bar and restaurant. 2nd District, Taborstrasse 12; Tel. 211 50-0; daily 12.00–14.30, 18.00–20.00
Hotel Biedermeier im Sünnhof. Café, "Zu den Deutschmeistern" restaurant, "Weissgärberstube" pub, as well as a Heurige cellar. 3rd District, Landstrasser Hauptstrasse 28; Tel. 716 71-0; café daily 6.30–22.30; restaurant daily 11.00–14.00, 18.00–20.00; pub daily 11.00–22.30 (with solid Viennese cuisine); Heurige, Tuesdays–Saturdays 17.00–1.00
Altes Presshaus Grinzing – Familie Krischke. 19th District, Cobenzlgasse 15; Tel. 320 02 03; daily 16.00–24.00

Erotic Vienna

Sexworld. Inviting sex shop, used by women more frequently than others. 6th District, Mariahilfer Strasse 49; Mondays–Fridays 10.00–20.00, Saturdays 10.00–17.00
Boudoir. Shop for bed-linen with erotic prints, and other accessories for every day love-making; also fitted out one of Elton John's residences. 9th District, Berggasse 14, Tuesdays–Fridays 10.00–18.30, Saturdays 10.00–13.00
Tiberius. One of the top addresses for lacquer, leather and rubber wear. 7th District, Lindengasse 2a; Mondays–Fridays 15.00–18.30, Saturdays 11.00–15.00
Erotic Center Naschmarkt. Peep-show and live couples, Mondays–Fridays 15.00, 17.00, 19.00 in the cinema, 14.00 and 18.00 in the peep-show. 4th District, Rechte Wienzeile 21; Mondays–Saturdays 9.00–22.00, Sundays, public holidays 12.00–22.00
The Big Apple. Go-go-shows on several stages and in a cage, also with male dancers and strippers for a female clientele. 1st District, Seilerstätte 5; daily 21.00–4.00
Hotel Orient. The most attractive and most famous hotel for "short stays"; a city legend, with a bar where you can easily drop in just to feel the atmosphere. 1st District, Tiefer Graben 30-32; Tel. 533 72 07
Josephine. Famous brothel in the Mutzenbacher-Haus, where men are pampered along the lines of the literary original (*Josephine Mutzenbacher* is a classic of Viennese erotic literature). 1st District, Sonnenfelsgasse 9; Tel. 512 93 69; Mondays–Saturdays 11.00–4.00, Sundays 20.00–4.00
City walk. "Josephine Mutzenbacher – in the footsteps of desire in old Vienna"; Tel. 712 98 49 (see also the current Wiener Spaziergänge (Vienna Walks) Brochure, available in any Tourist Information Office)
Red light district. Both sides of the Gürtel, particularly between Währinger Gürtel and the Westbahnhof; street prostitutes, bars, clubs, sex shops.

Vienna Online – 10 electronic excursions

Search engine Austronaut. This search machine provides a lot of Austria-specific web sites.<http://www.austronaut.at/>
wien online. The city of Vienna's web service with more than 4,000 pages and a dozen databases (timetables, swimming pool opening times, address searches and other Vienna information).<http://www.magwien.gv.at/>
Electronic timetable information. Enter the place and time of departure and the destination and you will obtain all route alternatives, the services to be used, stops at which to change and the duration of the trip for all Vienna's public transport services. <http://www.wiennet.at/efa/>
Austrian National Library. Several hundred pages of information (catalogue, special collections and history) elegantly presented as appropriate for a former Imperial Library. <http://www.onbac.at/>
Austrian Federal Museums online. This presents a good survey of current exhibitions in the large museums (Natural History Museum, Museum of Fine Arts, Museum of Modern Art Ludwig Foundation Vienna, etc.). <http://www.nhm-wien.ac.at/bundesmuseen/>
"Falter" city newspaper. Vienna's programme and events calendar. <http://www.vienna.at/Falter/>
Café Stein internet bar. 4 computers for surfing in the Internet; price: ATS 65.- for 30 minutes; daily 10.00–23.00, free advice on Wednesdays, Fridays and Sundays 17.00–23.00. 9th District, Währinger Strasse 6; Tel. 319 72 41.
Public Netbase tO Media-Space. Public access to the Internet, events in the net and many other activities. Mondays–Fridays 14.00–19.00, base lounge (meeting place) every Thursday from 21.00. 7th District, Museumsplatz 1, Museum Quarter, stair 5/Mezzanine; Tel. 523 58 81. homepage also in English. <http://www.t0.or.at/>
Cicero. An online source of information for Vienna's cultural and leisure programme; also in English. <http://www.vienna.cicero.net/>
Vienna Online. A server with lots of information about Vienna: news, weather, events and chatroom. <http://www.vienna.at/>, chatroom: <http://www.vienna.at/tmh/chat/>

1st edition 1998

Layout and jacket design by Andrea Schraml.
Editor of the German version: Michael Ponstingl.
Research: Alexander Uitz.
Translation by David Wright
Producer: Josef Embacher.
Photographic productions by Krammer Repro in Linz, Upper Austria.
Print: Studio Europa, Trient, Italy.

Illustration credits:
Austrian Archives/Dr. Christian Brandstätter, Vienna: p. 22, 104
Dagmar Landova, Vienna: p. 144
Verlag Christian Brandstätter, Bildarchiv:
p. 14, 15, 16, 17, 18, 28, 49, 143, 145

Copyright © 1998 by Verlag Christian Brandstätter, Vienna

All rights reserved. This book may not be reproduced or transmitted,
in whole or in part, in any form or by any means, electronic or mechanical,
including photocopy, translations, recording, microfilm
or any other information storage and retrieval system,
without prior written permission from the
Christian Brandstätter Verlagsgesellschaft m.b.H.
ISBN 3-85447-803-8

Christian Brandstätter Verlagsgesellschaft m.b.H.
A-1080 Wien, Wickenburggasse 26
Telephone (+43-1) 408 38 14
Fax (+43-1) 408 72 00
E-Mail: books@cbv.co.at